The
FINANCIALLY
SMART
DIVORCE

The

FINANCIALLY
SMART
DIVORCE

Three Steps to Your Ideal Settlement
and Financial Security in Your New Life

J.A. LICCIARDELLO, CDFA™

CERTIFIED DIVORCE FINANCIAL ANALYST

The Financially Smart Divorce

Copyright © 2016 by J. A. Licciardello. All Rights Reserved.

For information about this title or to order other books and/or electronic media, contact the publisher:

Wentworth Publishing
www.wentworthdivorceconsultants.com
wentworthplanning@gmail.com

Library of Congress Control Number: 2016906638

ISBN: 978-0-9962119-0-1 (print)
        978-0-9962119-1-8 (eBook)

Printed in the United States of America

Cover and Interior design: 1106 Design

Dedication

This book is dedicated to all the people who have gone through divorce and come out the other side with love in their hearts for their children and themselves, and respect for the person they were once married to.

I want to thank my children and their mother for their undying support which helped me take a little book idea and make it a reality.

$1 from every book sold will be donated to Sojourner House, a place where victims of domestic violence can be safe and begin rebuilding their lives.

Table of Contents

Stage 2—Negotiating An Agreement Right For You

Stage 3—Financial Recovery

Get on Track and Stay on Track
Throughout Your Divorce

Download the Free
"Financially Smart Divorce Planner"

This companion guide gives you everything you need to
implement the strategies in this book and stay
organized from start to finish.

Bonus content and tracking tools give you a clear path
to follow in building your ideal settlement and
future financial security.

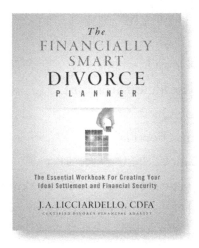

Download it now by clicking here or going to
www.wentworthdivorceconsultants.com/freefinancialplanner

Introduction

"Sheila's Story"

S heila is a friend of mine. Ivy League educated, she is a woman of great intellect and capabilities. She married a young medical student, David, who became a very successful physician. They had three young children, a beautiful home by the water, and fulfilling careers. Anyone looking at her life would say she had it all.

But her close friends knew it was not all a bed of roses. The marriage had become stale and the love simply wasn't there any longer. Her husband chose to move out first and got an apartment nearby. They shared time with the children, but it was clear that a divorce was in their future.

Financially she was in good shape, or so it would seem, as there was a lot of income between the two of them, and significant assets. And it appeared they cared about their children's welfare. So they each hired lawyers and began down the long path through the maze of divorce.

Amid the pain and upset, Sheila was relieved that her husband was willing to go along with the idea of her staying in the house with the kids. She loved her home as it was near the water and on a perfect little one-way street in a very desirable neighborhood. Maybe this experience wouldn't be so horrible after all.

Unfortunately, what followed was what many would call a typical divorce experience. The lawyers battled back and forth over points as basic as alimony support and as trivial as when child handoffs would occur. Along the way Sheila lost her job and picked up another one briefly only to lose it again. It was a confusing maelstrom of conflicting advice, meetings with lawyers, and incremental steps down an undefined path.

Sheila was feeling completely overwhelmed by the experience. She felt she would be okay money-wise, or at least hoped she would, but there was no clarity about what she needed to be financially secure. She was leaving it to her lawyer to tell her whether a financial proposal was good for her or not. But seeing the big picture and getting a sense of what her life would actually look like after her divorce was difficult, and the long-term outlook seemed impossible to gauge.

Despite little direct communication, after ten months of legal wrangling (and $35,000 in legal bills) they had an agreement that seemed workable. They went to court and had their divorce agreement approved. Sheila would stay in the house, get about 52 percent of mostly retirement assets and stock options, and have the children with her 70 percent of the time.

So the agreement was complete, but there was a lot to do to make it a reality. Accounts had to be opened, wills updated, insurance purchased, and she had no idea what to do with her investment money. Getting it all buttoned up was a huge undertaking, and it seemed to take forever to get the funds she was owed. Sheila was afraid she would forget to do something important.

Financially, Sheila was feeling the pinch. There was a roof to fix, a balky heating system, and just more rooms than she needed. So she decided to sell the house and get a smaller place. The costs to fix up the property and make it ready for sale ate into her liquid cash, and she began taking money out of her retirement accounts even though the taxes and penalties were substantial.

Credit was another issue. Because the house had been bought and owned by her former husband, Sheila had little credit history and found getting a mortgage to be a problem. She would need to have six months of child support history, and ideally a job, to get a mortgage.

She had neither.

At every turn there seemed to be another unforeseen obstacle, and she began to wonder during her sleep-deprived nights how long it would take before life felt normal again.

Does this sound familiar?

I wrote this book to give people like Sheila a step-by-step process to follow that will help them make financial settlements that work best for them and their families and avoid the mistakes that can compromise their financial futures.

My hope is that it will give you a path to follow so you can build a financial settlement right for you, gain peace of mind, and get the fresh start you deserve.

CHAPTER 1

The Problem with Divorce Today

"Marriage...the leading cause of divorce."
—*Groucho Marx*

Divorce is the largest financial transaction you will make in your lifetime. You need to get it right. Yet many people make agreements that are seriously flawed, leaving them in financial hardship and threatening their plans for the future.

But the simple fact that you picked up this book means you are already ahead of the game and have increased your odds of having a successful divorce; one where you start your new life off financially and emotionally whole. In the following pages you will be given a path to follow that will help you make financial decisions based on what you need most to be happy in your new life, and avoid disastrous mistakes.

This book deals with all things financial in divorce. You will receive information on getting organized, dividing assets properly, keeping or selling the family home, child support and alimony, handling complex assets and many other topics. I also put a spotlight on the biggest mistakes to avoid, and time-tested strategies you should consider to help you build a great settlement. Lastly, you will have a blueprint for reconstructing your new financial life the right way. From preparation to recovery it's in here.

The Problem with Divorce—By the Numbers

One would hope that there would be a finely tuned legal system in place that creates well designed agreements for couples that are generally reasonable people. But the truth is that the divorce system is a mess, and financial settlements are often not balanced and fair. They frequently enrich one spouse, while the other suffers a significant reduction in lifestyle and a loss of financial security. So the next few pages talk about why the system doesn't work well and what can be done to fix it. But feel free to move to the part that talks about whether you should have a financial coach. What you miss will not be on the test.

The first step in fixing anything is to fully understand the problem. But, as I began the research for this book, I came across very few statistics that described how people felt about their divorce experience. So I commissioned a study to find out.[1]

---

1   Survey conducted November 2014 by Wentworth Divorce Consultants through Survata Inc., Survey asked 402 divorced individuals about their divorce processes and experiences. Respondents were balanced by age, geography, sex, and economic background.

Here are some statistics from respondents who divorced the traditional way (litigation):

- 💰 32% were dissatisfied with their financial settlement.

- 💰 43% found the divorce process worsened their relationship with their spouse.

- 💰 76% looked only to their lawyer for financial advice.

- 💰 77% wished they had worked with a financial specialist throughout their divorce.

This survey further showed that it didn't matter what method people used to get divorced. Even if they chose to go the route of non-confrontation through using mediation or a collaborative divorce process, many were unhappy with the results.[2]

So what explains these troubling statistics? In my humble opinion I think the industry suffers from a bad case of "divorce financial blindness."

Divorce Financial Blindness

Divorce financial blindness is what happens when people don't have the information they need to make sound decisions and instead make choices based on expediency, emotion, and incomplete consideration of the alternatives.

---

2   A quick look at these numbers suggests that the legal community is falling short in servicing the needs of divorcing couples. Perhaps. But one survey doesn't tell the whole story, and I know personally many lawyers who are caring, ethical, and intelligent professionals.

Divorce Financial Blindness occurs because of four factors:

- 💰 A process that doesn't promote clarity

- 💰 Poor financial preparation

- 💰 Blind decision-making during negotiations

- 💰 The lack of a well-built and monitored recovery plan after divorce

The Divorce Process

People make bad decisions when they are under stress, and divorce can be an emotionally challenging experience. The perceived urgency to make decisions under deadline makes it easy to build a settlement that is a hodgepodge of asset divisions and financial commitments.

Every approach to divorce has its flaws. In a mediated divorce the free-flowing nature of discussions creates the potential for glossing over important financial facts and circumstances.[3] And in a litigated divorce, attorneys often feel an obligation to advocate for their clients in a win/lose atmosphere, potentially creating conflict between spouses and needless billable hours. Financial clarity is lost in the noise.

Poor Preparation

As you will see in this book, there is a lot to do to become fully prepared for divorce negotiations.

One of my big gripes about the divorce business is that there is little focus on doing the upfront work needed to ensure settlements are designed

---

3   For more information on this topic, please read my article, "Maintaining Financial Integrity in the Mediated Divorce." It can be found at my website www.wentworthdivorceconsultants.com.

properly. As a result many divorcing couples are unclear about the strengths and weaknesses of their finances in the context of getting divorced, and even less clear about what they need for their future single life. Fewer still have a grasp of more complicated considerations, such as the impact of taxes, the proper valuation of pension plans and business interests, and potential credit issues.

Blind Decision-Making

It may be hard to believe but most divorce financial decisions are made without actually running the numbers. Instead they are made by gut feel.

It is simply impossible to decide between two financial alternatives if you can't compare the benefits of each. So decisions such as whether one spouse should keep the marital home while the other gets the pension are left to intuition and emotion—with potentially disastrous consequences.

It also may come as a surprise to learn that lawyers, mediators, and judges are **not** obligated to ensure every reasonable financial proposal is offered and evaluated on its merits. Comparing alternative asset divisions and illustrating to clients how their financial lives may be affected is simply not a required part of the process. It is hard to fathom, but true.

Lastly, while most people look to their lawyers for financial guidance, many attorneys do not have the expertise or financial tools to do the job properly.

The Lack of a Financial Recovery Plan

Once the divorce agreement is finalized there is a natural tendency for everyone to exhale a little and begin focusing on finding a place to live, getting the kids resettled, and "moving on." But it is at this point—implementing the agreement in real life—that so many mistakes are made.

Accounts need to be opened, budgets established, assets transferred, insurance reviewed, and investment strategies designed, to name just a few of the tasks involved. Unfortunately, just when these crucial steps need to be taken, many lawyers and mediators have moved on to their next client engagement.

A Time for Change

I don't pretend to have all the answers, but I believe divorce financial blindness can be cured if couples use a fundamentally different approach to ending their marriage. One where they methodically identify their priorities, assess their options, and construct their settlement using logic, not emotion.

While divorce is often not a pleasant experience there is no requirement for it to be an expensive and contentious battle with winners and losers and lifelong damage to relationships. Instead,

> *Divorce should be a thoughtful negotiation where an agreement is formed based on the needs of each spouse (and any children) and a careful review of the alternatives.*

Now I know this may sound like an over-optimistic vision. It isn't. In fact more and more people are choosing mediation and other alternatives to litigation to exit their marriage with less cost and reduced conflict. What is missing is an instruction manual that shows people how to be effective participants, and a process that is well-designed and easy to follow.

In the following chapters you will be given a program for making smart financial decisions through each stage of your divorce, from preparation to recovery. You will have a step-by-step path to follow to build a settlement right for you.

We also show you how a divorce financial specialist might be used to clarify complex issues, and help you make fully informed decisions. In the next section we describe what they do and how to decide if they should be part of your advisor team. In the interest of full disclosure it is the work we do at our firm.

The Certified Divorce Financial Analyst

In recent years there has been increased use of financial experts among divorcing couples and individuals looking to build superior settlements.

They have many titles but the Certified Divorce Financial Analyst, or CDFA™, is the most well known. The CDFA™ designation is granted by the Institute for Divorce Financial Analysts (IDFA) to those experienced financial planners who have taken advanced courses and passed an extensive set of exams on the intricacies of divorce finance.

A CDFA™ works with you alone or together with your spouse. They can participate as a neutral financial expert in mediation, or assist you and your attorney as needed in a litigated divorce. They use advanced divorce financial software[4] to show you how each financial proposal may affect

---

4   Such as Family Law Software. More information can be found at http://www.familylaw software.com/.

you years down the road, and can summarize your entire settlement in easy-to-understand terms prior to your approval.

A CDFA™ helps you:

- 💰 Organize your financial information

- 💰 Prepare a game plan for negotiations based on your priorities and financial realities

- 💰 Account for taxes, inflation, and penalties that can reduce the true value of an asset

- 💰 Work through thorny financial decisions that arise during negotiations

- 💰 Build a balanced and fair settlement that is right for you

- 💰 Structure alimony and child support in the most advantageous way

- 💰 See clearly how your settlement will affect your financial life many years out

- 💰 Ensure paperwork is filed properly to transfer assets

- 💰 Implement a financial recovery plan and get your new financial life organized the right way.

Should You Hire a CDFA™?

Like any hiring decision you need to look at the costs and the benefits.

A fee-based divorce financial advisor will cost you anywhere from $100 to $200 per hour—less than your lawyer most likely—and some will work on a flat fee.

You can expect that you will have 5 to 10 hours of billable time depending on the complexity of your finances and the level of assistance you require. Your CDFA™ should be able to give you an estimate of what his or her services are likely to cost in advance.

There are other people skilled in the area of divorce finance, including some lawyers and certified public accountants (CPAs), and a variety of financial professionals. Whomever you choose, he or she absolutely needs to be able to able to run specialized financial analyses using software designed for divorce and charge you on a fee basis, not as part of a future product sale. You want unbiased advice.

Not everyone going through divorce needs a financial expert on their team. But the more complex your finances the more value they can provide. In the following chapters I highlight what a CDFA™ or other financial coach might do to help you throughout your divorce so you can decide whether you should consider using one.

In this book I use the terms CDFA™, financial coach and financial analyst interchangeably to describe a financial expert specializing in divorce.

CHAPTER 2

The Three Stages of Divorce

"Sometimes the right path is not the easiest one."
—*Pocahontas*

In the previous chapter I pointed out that our system of divorce does not automatically create fair settlements, and people are financially blind and make bad decisions. So, how do you go about fixing it?

I believe divorce needs to be viewed not as a single event but as a much longer-lasting process beginning with marital disenchantment and ending with emotional and financial recovery.

Rather than an event that hits like a blizzard in January, it is more the passing of a season. It often starts well before the lawyer or mediator is called, perhaps in the therapist's office or the Wednesday reading group, and ends far after the final papers are received in the mail.

Therefore, I have split this book into three simple stages—*preparation, negotiation, and recovery*—and offer strategies and tools for managing each effectively.

Everyone goes through these steps, phases, stages, or whatever you wish to call them. Unfortunately, many people simply get on the divorce train and go for a ride, making decisions as they present themselves.

But being a casual participant in your divorce is dangerous. If you don't follow some kind of plan to make good financial decisions during divorce you might:

- Create a settlement that looks good on day one but horrible five years later

- Not have enough income to support your future lifestyle

- Endure unfocused negotiations that seem to go on forever

- Spend much more money than necessary in mediation and legal services

- Make bad financial decisions because you don't have the analyses you need to see your financial future in stark clarity

- Sign an agreement that looks good on paper but is really flawed in some way

- Not do the critical things needed to ensure your family's financial security once your divorce is over.

If there were ever a time to take charge it is now. You will benefit by helping drive the divorce train.

The Three Stages of Divorce

This book is broken down into three stages: preparation, negotiation, and recovery.

Preparation Assessing your goals, taking a realistic look at your financial life, and developing priorities so you negotiate the things that are most important to your long-term well-being and make sensible financial decisions for yourself and your family.

Negotiation Dealing effectively with the task of creating the terms of your divorce and designing a financial settlement that, in its entirety, is fair and equitable to you.

Recovery Moving beyond the divorce into your new life and getting your finances rebuilt in a way that supports your goals as a single person.[5]

Each stage is important. One is not more important than the other. If you prepare improperly you may end up negotiating things that are not your highest priority. Poor negotiation may result in an agreement that is unfair and inequitable. And not getting your finances rebuilt properly during the recovery phase can make even a good agreement fall flat on its face.

---

5 Healing psychologically is also required to feel fully recovered. I recommend reading *The Complete Divorce Recovery Handbook* by John P. Splinter (Grand Rapids, Mich.: Zondervan, 1992).

If you prepare thoroughly, negotiate skillfully what you need the most, and rebuild your finances the right way, you will have the best chance for divorce financial success.

How This Book Is Organized to Help You

This book is organized around these three distinct stages of exiting your marriage, with strategies and tools for handling each one effectively.

My goal is not only to bring you up to speed on important divorce finance topics, but to *give you an action plan to follow*. The plan includes:

- Specific tips and action items in each chapter so you know what to focus on

- The most common mistakes people make along the way

- A step-by-step set of exercises and tools found at the back of this book and on my website so you end each stage ready to move on to the next

- Reports and analyses you may want to have a divorce financial analyst (or "financial coach" as I refer to them) prepare for you to help you make informed decisions.

Download the Free "Financially Smart Divorce Planner"

I have created a companion guide to *The Financially Smart Divorce* so you can put into action the concepts and exercises described in this book.

It has full size versions of the checklists and questionnaires plus bonus content including:

- A Guide on how to compare and choose between alternative proposals

- 24 questions to help you create a game plan for negotiations

- 30 questions that will help you identify what you need most in your settlement

- A "countdown to launch" sequence that ensures you are truly ready to sign your settlement

- An "Agreement Tracker" spreadsheet to help you implement your financial agreement

- Reports and analyses that can simplify your decision making

And it is completely free for people who have bought *The Financially Smart Divorce.*

Just click here if you have the ebook version or go to www.wentworth divorceconsultants.com/freefinancialplanner/ and you will have all that you need to manage your divorce properly from start to finish.

Let's get going down the path by getting you started with Stage 1... "Preparation."

STAGE 1

Preparation

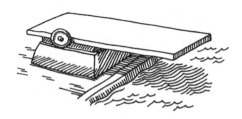

CHAPTER 3

The Decision to Exit
Your Marriage

"When two people decide to get a divorce, it isn't a sign that they 'don't understand' one another, but a sign that they have, at last, begun to."
—Helen Rowland

Choosing to divorce can be a difficult decision. The prospect of a major change in lifestyle, relationships, and finances can make a person's head spin with uncertainty even if fixing the marriage seems impossible. Many couples simply carry on and try to keep up appearances. We all know them.

Statistics don't lie (usually), and recent research has revealed that one in five people, especially women, feel stuck in an unhappy marriage but will not divorce for fear of financial hardship.[6]

---

6   Survey (conducted in 2014) of 2,000 married adults in the UK by the law firm Slater and Gordon.

My friends in the therapist community agree with this statistic, saying that for many of their divorcing patients financial anxieties are near the top of the list.

These concerns manifest themselves in the form of many questions:

- 💰 Can I withstand the change to a potentially less affluent lifestyle?

- 💰 Will I have to uproot the children (if any) by selling the house?

- 💰 Can I afford to pay child support and alimony?

- 💰 Will I have to abandon my plans for retirement?

- 💰 Will I need to get a new job or start working?

- 💰 Is it worth staying in the marriage simply for the financial security?

One of the flaws in the divorce process is that there is no easy way for people to assess the financial side of the divorce decision. The result is that they stay in a place of fear and uncertainty, hoping that problems will fix themselves, or jump into divorce mode and hope for the best.

I propose another approach, where people get the answers they need to feel completely informed about the financial part of their decision to divorce. It is formally called the pre-divorce financial assessment, but I like to refer to it as the "financial reality check."

The Pre-Divorce Financial Reality Check

Seeing how your family's finances would look as two separate households is not as easy as taking your assets and dividing by two. You can't easily split a house in half (although some have tried), and there are many considerations that dictate what a court might find "fair and equitable" in your settlement.

What the assessment gives you is a view of your future finances so you can make a divorce decision with confidence. It is an analysis run by a divorce financial analyst to project how your financial life may change in terms of cash flow, savings, net worth, and other measures of financial health.

The assessment is built on many assumptions which you can adjust to generate potential best- and worst-case scenarios. You can easily create "what-if" reports to see how changes in any aspect of your finances affect you years down the road. All in all you get a clearer view of your future so you can make choices based on what is right for you and your family.

Divorce Financial Facts

There is no way of knowing precisely what your settlement agreement will look like should you divorce, but there are some overall facts about finances that apply to almost everyone.

Getting Divorced Costs Money

Divorce costs money in the form of professionals needed to get your agreements negotiated and implemented, and get you re-established in your new life. These people include:

- 💰 Lawyers

- 💰 Mediators

- Appraisers

- Real estate agents

- CPAs or tax specialists

- Business valuation specialists

- Pension valuation specialists

- Financial specialists

- Parenting specialists

- Therapists

The simpler your finances the lower the costs are likely to be. But a divorce where one spouse owns a business or participates in complex executive compensation or pension programs will cost you more.

Taxes Can Take a Bite Out of Your Assets

Investments such as your home and stock portfolio may be subject to taxes if they need to be sold. With few exceptions there will be some tax money sent to state and federal governments if they are liquidated. You may also have higher tax rates after divorce, as you lose the opportunity to file jointly as a married couple. You will get more information in chapter 14 on taxes and their impact on asset values in divorce.

Living Expenses Rise

You can expect your cost of living to rise if you split one household into two. It is just a fact of life.

Some Assets May Not Be Available Right Away

Some assets may be delayed in getting to you due to paperwork or other issues. Selling a home doesn't happen instantly. Splitting retirement plans require special paperwork to be drawn up and can take months to be acted upon by the employer. And some assets like pensions may even require a former spouse to retire before being received.

The Length of Your Marriage Matters

If you earn less than your former spouse, you are entitled to half of your ex's Social Security benefits if it exceeds what you have based on your own earnings record…if your marriage lasts ten years or more. This is talked about more in chapter 16.

Making the Decision

There is much written about how to know if your marriage is really over. As the author of this book, I can't weigh in with an opinion as to what is best for you. But, as a divorced person who has been in the single world for ten years now, I will tell you that it is a decision that demands a mixture of pragmatism and a keen awareness about what nurtures your soul.

Therapists can help you with what is possible in the relationship and what is good for you as an individual. My suggestion to you is to combine this with a clear view of how your future may look financially and make a decision that works on all levels.

Of course no one deserves to be in an abusive relationship, and there are times when a quick exit is called for; but for most people there is value in taking time to make a measured assessment and leaving only when it makes complete sense to do so. You will then know in both your heart and mind that the time is right to move on.

Hang in there. It does get better.

Actions to Take Now

If you are still considering divorce and have financial questions, you should consider a "pre-divorce financial assessment." Your therapist may be able to recommend someone, or you can call us at Wentworth Divorce Consultants and we will be glad to help you or refer you to someone who can.

CHAPTER 4

Deciding How to Divorce

"Intelligence is quickness in seeing things as they are."
—*George Santayana*

If you watch old movies about divorce you will often see emotional court-room scenes where a husband or wife is threatened with losing "everything."[7] Accusations fly, gavels are slammed, and grand pronouncements are made sending one spouse away wealthy, and the other to the poorhouse. Fortunately it has little to do with the way most divorces are conducted today.

One of the more exciting trends in the world of marital law is the emergence of alternatives to the traditional litigated and adversarial divorce. Whether it is to save money, preserve relationships, or keep matters private, more couples are opting to use mediators or other alternative approaches to work out their settlement.

---

7   I highly recommend the movie "All of Me" with Steve Martin and Lily Tomlin for the courtroom scene. Check it out on youtube.

As I mentioned earlier, my firm conducted a national survey to find out what method people were choosing to get divorced. One trend became clear: people are moving away from using lawyers in a traditional litigated divorce and toward mediation, collaboration, and the do-it-yourself divorce process.

While experiences varied, couples were more satisfied with their settlements and had better relationships with their ex-spouses when they opted to work cooperatively through mediation and other alternatives to litigation. So let's take a closer look at each.

Traditional Litigation

A traditional contested divorce is court-centered, with laws and procedures governing the process. If spouses cannot come to an agreement, a judge may be forced to make final decisions for the couple regarding financial and parenting issues.

Most divorcing couples settle outside the courtroom, but settlements are designed in preparation for trial. This means spouses may be positioned as opponents and the entire proceeding may have an adversarial tone. This can obviously be counterproductive to couples who are looking to work cooperatively in settling their divorce.

Having said that, sometimes an agreement can only be reached through the court process, especially if there are entrenched disagreements or a lack of trust.

Mediation

Mediation is the process where you and your spouse create an agreement cooperatively with the assistance of a neutral third party: the mediator.

There are typically no lawyers present; it is simply a mediator professionally trained in divorce and conflict resolution working with the couple to build an agreement. If issues arise that require an outside expert, the mediator brings in a neutral specialist to render an opinion.

At the end of the process, a marital settlement outline is drafted[8] (often called a memorandum of understanding) and the parties will typically have it reviewed by their attorneys to make certain that the language reflects what they intended.

Once it is independently confirmed that the agreement is what the couple have agreed to, it is signed and notarized. When fully executed it is presented to a judge for his or her approval.

Collaborative Divorce

In a collaborative divorce each party is represented by an attorney who is trained in the collaborative process.

The attorneys and their respective clients enter into a fee agreement that positions each attorney as a legal advisor and facilitator in designing win-win agreements. If the collaborative process is unsuccessful, the attorneys agree to not represent the parties should the matter go to litigation.

Often there are a number of advisors who are involved in the process. These may include child care specialists, CDFAs™, therapists, and other experts.

---

8   If the mediator is not an attorney, he or she will create a memorandum of understanding, which an attorney will then rewrite to contain the legally binding language that a judge can approve. I always recommend having an attorney review all agreements prior to submission to court.

The Do-It-Yourself, Pro Se Divorce

An increasing number of Americans are choosing to bypass the traditional methods of divorce in favor of doing it themselves. Fully 32 percent of couples divorcing in the last five years chose to use this approach versus mediation, litigation, or collaborative methods.[9]

This approach, called *pro se* after the Latin term meaning to "appear for oneself," is a lower-cost method of getting divorced because many tasks that would traditionally be handled by a lawyer are completed by you or your spouse.

Of course, the potential benefits need to be weighed against the potential costs, which include:

- Not having a legal professional to ensure your rights are protected

- The potential for agreeing to a financial settlement that is not truly fair and equitable

- Having an incomplete or faulty parenting agreement that requires continuous court appearances to finalize.

> *Divorce is complicated and mistakes can be costly.*
> *You should consult an attorney to understand*
> *the potential risks of representing yourself in court.*

---

9   National survey conducted November 2014 by Wentworth Divorce Financial Advisors.

Which Method Is Right for You?

In deciding which approach to take, there are a number of considerations, including your ability to work with your spouse, the level of trust in the relationship, cost, and the complexity of your marital finances.

🪙 How cooperatively can you and your spouse work together?

It is a myth that you need to have an exceptionally cooperative relationship with your spouse for mediation or collaborative divorce to work. Conflict and disagreement are almost always a part of the process, and a skilled mediator can help you work through issues and arrive at solutions you both can agree to.

Mediation, however, will not work where one spouse is intent on winning at all costs and attempts to reduce your bargaining power by dominating every meeting. My suggestion is that if you think there is a chance you can work together, give mediation a try. Your mediator will be able to gauge early on whether your talks will be productive and fair.

It should be noted that many couples choose to use mediation initially to build the parts of their settlement they can agree on, and then work through their attorneys to work out the remaining issues.

🜚 Can you trust your spouse to be honest about his or her finances?

One of the benefits of a litigated court proceeding is that there is a formal "discovery" process that requires all parties to fully and accurately disclose their finances under penalty of perjury. If you feel there is the possibility your spouse may try to gain an advantage by fudging the numbers, litigation may be your best option.

🜚 Cost

Litigation and collaborative divorce are the more expensive options due to the number of legal hours billed. Mediation tends to be lower cost, and pro se the least costly. But you have to factor in whether you will arrive at a settlement that is fair to you. A cheap divorce that results in a bad settlement is not a smart option financially.

🜚 Financial complexity

If you have assets such as business interests, rental properties, executive compensation or pensions, you will need specialized analyses to make an informed decision. And, if there are questions about whether an asset owned prior to the marriage is a marital asset subject to division, you will want professional legal and financial guidance.

Your team will need to include a CDFA™, CPA, lawyer, and other specialists to help you evaluate alternatives in dividing assets. All approaches can provide this level of expertise, but in general the more complex the finances the more likely you will need the regular services of your lawyer and the protections the litigated process provides.

> *I recommend you always consult with an attorney before*
> *your agreement is finalized. You need to know your rights,*
> *be familiar with how the divorce process works in your*
> *state, and verify that your settlement is worded so that it*
> *accurately represents what you have agreed to.*

I have included in the workbook section a chart that compares in detail the litigation, mediation, and collaborative methods to getting divorced. You will want to check with your state's practices with regard to the pro se approach.

Actions to Take Now

- Review the options and consider the pros and cons of each one. If you have downloaded the implementation guide you will see a complete comparison of each method.

- Reflect on whether an alternative approach to litigation such as mediation is likely to be productive, given you and your spouse's ability to work cooperatively in creating a fair agreement.

- Speak with an attorney and mediator to learn more about their roles in each approach.

- Choose an option that works best for you.

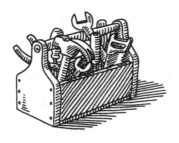

CHAPTER 5

Preparing to Make Good Financial Decisions

"When you're prepared, you're more confident.
When you have a strategy, you're more comfortable."
—Fred Couples

I like to cook and sometimes don't follow a recipe just for the adventure of it. I lay out all my ingredients like they do on the cooking shows, pour a glass of wine and go at it. Sometimes I create something memorable, sometimes not so much. But it doesn't matter. I always end up with something edible, and the fun is in the preparation.

Now, divorce is not creating curried chicken soup with homemade noodles.[10] There is a lot more on the line. Poor decision-making can lead

---

10   One of the experiments that worked. Email me and I will give you the recipe.

to unnecessary financial hardship and affect every one of your short- and long-term financial goals.

The first step on the path toward financial security after divorce is getting properly prepared. And I don't mean just getting your financial records together for your lawyer to review. I mean *really, fully, completely* prepared! Soup to nuts.

This chapter will help you understand whether you are ready to begin negotiations or whether you need to bone up on some parts of divorce personal finance.

It all starts with the Financial Readiness Scorecard.

The Financial Readiness Scorecard

Personal finance is an area that most people don't pay much attention to day-to-day. Jobs, children, and putting food on the table demand more attention than our credit score or whether we have adequate insurance.

Divorce requires that you have a handle on a broad array of financial topics…from estate planning to taxes to how Social Security works. The readiness test helps you understand your knowledge gaps and give you insights into:

- How well you know your family's personal finances

- How well you have defined your vision for the future

- How your financial life will be affected by your divorce.

It is a self-assessment so, as you have heard many times, there are no right or wrong answers. Use it to gauge how much preparation you will need to negotiate your divorce settlement and whether a financial coach would be helpful to you.

The scorecard can be found in the back of this book, and printable, full-size versions can be found in the free financial planner available via download at www.divorcefinancialally.com/freefinancialplanner.

Scoring the Financial Readiness Scorecard

Each question is answered on a ten-point scale. The higher the rating you give yourself the more you feel prepared to deal with that particular financial aspect of your divorce. Simply circle the number that best matches your self-assessment.

You will likely find some variation in what you know; perhaps you are familiar with investing strategies but not estate planning issues. That is to be expected. The point is to identify your financial blind spots and clarify where assistance or research may be most helpful to you.

On the page following the readiness test you will see a place for you to note the three questions you scored lowest. Take a moment and write down those three areas and consider what would be needed to have you score higher in each.

What to Do with the Results

Once you have determined where you need additional financial knowledge, you have three choices:

- *Pick up the knowledge you need through your own research* or rely on your attorney or spouse to help you as needed. This can be a good strategy if your finances are simple.

🛍 *Find a qualified divorce financial advisor to give you the analysis and guidance you need on an ad hoc basis.* This can be beneficial but requires you to recognize issues as they arise.

🛍 *Work with a financial coach through all three stages of your divorce from preparation to recovery.* It costs more but if your finances are complex it may be the best way to build a fair and balanced settlement and rebuild your finances once your divorce is final.

Actions to Take Now

🛍 Take the financial readiness test and score it. The free implementation guide has a full size copy of the questionnaire and scoring sheet.

🛍 Review the questions you scored lowest on and determine your knowledge gaps.

🛍 Decide if a CDFA™, or other financial coach, would be helpful to you or whether you can fill the gaps with your own research and analysis.

CHAPTER 6

Establishing Your Life Vision

"Would you tell me, please, which way I ought to go from here?"
"That depends a good deal on where you want to get to."
"I don't much care where—"
"Then it doesn't matter which way you go."
—*Lewis Carroll,* Alice in Wonderland

Divorce can be a roller coaster. For many people it is filled with rapid change, with decision after decision forced upon them. That is why you need to have a clear picture of what you want your life to look like after your divorce is over. You really do need a vision.

Really, a vision? If you have spent any time in the business world, or are a fan of the comic strip "Dilbert", you may think vision setting is a silly exercise that only pointy headed bosses do to drive their underlings crazy.

You may also be saying "My vision is to simply survive this ordeal!" I get that. But having a vision helps you to focus on the possibilities of a great future and makes you more powerful in your negotiations. It also allows you to make decisions based on what you need to live the life you want rather than on the whims of a judge or the needs of your spouse. It helps give you control.

Nothing is guaranteed, and sometimes financial realities will dictate a lifestyle that is not exactly what you want at first. But, if you have a vision framed in your mind, you will know what is required to make it a reality and naturally make the choices that will get you closer to your ideal life. As Stephen Covey said in his most famous book many years ago, "begin with the end in mind."[11]

There Are Three Parts to Your Vision

Your vision is simply a view of how you would like your life to be in three domains: lifestyle, relationships, and long-term goals.

Lifestyle Goals	This is where you envision how you want to live after your divorce is final. Do you wish to stay in the family home? What kind of parenting arrangement will you have with your ex-spouse? Will your children live with you full time? Will you work? What level of income will you need?

---

11   Stephen Covey, *The 7 Habits of Highly Effective People* (New York: Penguin, 1989).

Relationship Goals   What kind of relationship do you want to have with your spouse, your friends, and your children? What will success look like? Thinking this through will help you make the right decisions about whether mediation or another alternative to the courtroom is worth considering

Long-Term Goals   Now, I know thinking ahead to the next week can be a challenge during a divorce, but having a sense of where you want to be ten years down the road and beyond will help you make better decisions. What does retirement mean to you? What do you want your life to look like once the kids move out?

Answer the Lifestyle and Vision Questions

In the workbook section I have given you a list of twenty-two questions worth pondering. Take the time to quietly go through them and begin building an idea of what your ideal life will be like in the years after you are divorced. Begin with the end in mind.

Actions to Take Now

- Read through the vision questions and write down your answers to each one. If you have downloaded the implementation guide you will find these questions organized in a way to make it easier to develop your vision.

- 💰 Consolidate your answers. On the "Developing Your Vision" page, consolidate your answers into a short description of how your ideal life will look and feel.

- 💰 Make a Personal Action Plan. On the "Personal Action" page list the projects and actions most important for achieving your vision.

CHAPTER 7

Getting Organized

"Out of clutter, find simplicity.
From discord, find harmony.
In the middle of difficulty lies opportunity."
—*Albert Einstein*

My friend Barbara is a pack rat. Unlike me, who needs the spice rack alphabetized and gets excited around label makers, she is comfortable with vast amounts of clutter. She calls it casual living, I call it crazy.

Regardless of whether people are neat freaks or clutter freaks, or something in between, most live their financial lives in a state of semi-organization. The bills get paid and the credit cards managed, but many important activities fall out of their consciousness until they are completely forgotten.

I hate to even say this, but one of the good things about divorce is that you are forced to get up close and personal with all aspects of your finances. Early on in the process you must account for all of your assets, your debt, and your expenses. The court requires it.

This chapter gives you a process for getting organized and gathering the information you need for your financial disclosure forms.

This is also the time to take some defensive measures if you have less than complete trust in your spouse. So I have included a section with some tips on what you can do protect yourself.

Gather Your Records

One of the first actions you will take once the petition for divorce is filed is to provide a full and truthful accounting of your personal finances to your attorney and the court. You spouse will file one as well.

In the workbook section of this book you will see a Getting Organized Document Checklist to help you gather this information. It is broken down into a number of categories.

In each of these categories gather recent paper statements or go online and print off the information. You will consolidate all of this data into a summary to be forwarded to the court on their official forms, and to your attorney or mediator.

Cash

This is the money you use to pay the bills. Begin your data-gathering process by collecting statements for your bank checking and savings accounts. If you have a brokerage relationship you may also have cash there to be accounted for.

Investment and Retirement Accounts

Individual retirement accounts (IRAs) and certain insurance products like variable annuities are in this category, as are company retirement plans such as 401(k)s. You should receive quarterly mailings showing the value and portfolio details.

Corporate Compensation Plans

Employer plans such as stock purchase, stock option, and deferred compensation programs should also be accounted for. Lastly, don't forget about pension plans. You may have more difficulty getting this information as you probably don't receive a monthly statement. But they are required to report at least once a year on the accrued benefits.

Debt

Get a copy of your mortgage statement, home equity loans, car loans, and credit cards. Make a note of any loans on your 401(k) accounts as well.

Life Insurance Contracts

These are the core protections your family relies on should an income provider die unexpectedly. Some insurance contracts have cash value as well. Find the contract you were given when you opened up the policy or ask your insurance advisor to get you a copy from the insurance company.

Make a List of Your Personal Property

You should take an inventory of all of your personal property. Make note of those items that were owned before the marriage or received as gifts or inheritance. There will be a determination made during your divorce as to which of your belongings are subject to split as part of your financial settlement. This subject is talked about more in the next chapter on marital versus separate property.

Get a Copy Your Will and/or Trust Documents

The court will not need a copy of your will and other estate documents, but you will want to review them and assess whether changes should be made.

Review Beneficiary Designations

It is important to note that many of your assets are not distributed based on your will when you die. Jointly held assets such as a home and checking accounts, insurance products, and retirement accounts all have named beneficiaries and are passed on to your heirs outside of your will.

You will want to make a note of which of these assets name your spouse as beneficiary. It is likely that you will want to remove him or her after you are divorced, and perhaps sooner. Consult with your attorney before making changes.

Estimate Your Expenses and Income

This one is often an eye-opener. Most people don't know where their money goes or only have a fuzzy sense of their expenses. It is easy to remember the mortgage payment and the health club dues while forgetting the three-dollar-a-day Starbucks habit. It all counts.

A simple way to approach this most tedious of financial tasks is to go online and download a year's worth of activity from your bank and credit card companies into a spreadsheet. Most firms provide you a way of doing this. Sort it by the establishment name and you have an initial understanding of where your money goes.

One thing not accounted for is cash expenditures, but you will see ATM fees all bunched together, giving you an idea of how much of your spending is unaccounted for. Saving a month's worth of receipts will help you identify what you are doing with all that cash.

Separate and Modify Expenses Based on Your Future Life

Separate your expenses into categories as defined by the financial disclosure forms your state requires. You will need to modify some of these expenses based on what you expect them to be as a single person. Your costs for housing may change, as will perhaps health care expenses and home maintenance.

Getting this as accurate as possible is really important. In order for your financial settlement to be fair it needs to be based on reality. Missing an essential expense or underestimating by a wide margin what it will cost to support your lifestyle will make negotiations flawed from the outset. It is also problematic to overstate your expenses as your financial affidavit is an official court document and exposes you to potential penalties if it is discovered to be intentionally misleading.

Calculating Income

You need to account for all sources of income: from employment, taxable investments, alimony and child support from a previous marriage, Social Security...all of it.

You will also need to deconstruct your paycheck, and separate out the deductions and taxes that reduce your gross income and result in your take-home pay. Included may be deductions for health care premiums and other insurance, Social Security and Medicare, 401(k), and other savings plans.

So there is a little math required to understand what your income really is and to get all the data required on the mandatory court disclosure forms. But you should find it an enlightening exercise.

Defensive Maneuvers to Consider

While most divorcing spouses are honest and trustworthy, it is important to take prudent actions to protect yourself from maneuvers a spouse might take to get an unfair financial advantage.

Consider Putting Assets in Your Name Alone

Most families have joint accounts in both the husband's and wife's names. Spouses are not allowed to hide or dramatically spend down assets during a divorce proceeding. Nevertheless, if there is reason to believe your spouse is not trustworthy, it may be prudent to move some of these assets from your joint account into one in your name only.

Some advisors will suggest you move half of the joint assets to an account in your name alone, but this may be looked at unfavorably by your spouse and the courts. Your attorney can give you guidance on the wisdom of this action.

Review Wills, Trusts, and Insurance Policies

Most people take it for granted that their spouse won't make a change to the beneficiaries designated on these types of accounts. But it happens. Get fresh copies of these documents and make note of the current beneficiaries. They will need to be updated after your divorce is finalized.

Open a Credit Card in Your Name Only

Having a credit card in your name will help you establish your own individual credit history. Also, credit cards may help with day-to-day living expenses during the divorce when some of your other funds may be frozen or unavailable. Do this before any divorce proceedings start, especially if you are not working or if your income is substantially less than your spouse's.

Get a Copy of Your Credit Report

You should immediately get copies of your credit report. You want to be able to resolve any disputes as soon as possible. If you are concerned that your soon-to-be-ex spouse might borrow money in your name, you might want to sign up for a credit monitoring service. These services will notify you anytime there's a change to your credit history. Again, keep in mind that you are prohibited from aggressively spending down accounts or "dissipating" assets in an attempt to gain financial advantage.

Actions to Take Now

- Review the Getting Organized Document Checklist in the back of this book, or in the implementation guide you have downloaded.

- Gather your records as described in this chapter.

- Analyze your expenses and income sources.

- Consider taking the prescribed defensive maneuvers after consulting with your lawyer.

CHAPTER 8

Identifying What Assets Are Subject to Split

"Instead of getting married again, I'm just going to find a woman I don't like and give her a house."
—Lewis Grizzard

You would think some things would be simple in life. If you have been married a while, it might seem obvious to you what needs to be part of your marital settlement. But there are a host of rules, and laws, that define what is considered to be "marital property" and subject to division between you and your soon-to-be ex.

What state you live in, what kind of property it is, and how and when it was acquired are all factors in determining whether it is marital or separate property. Let's take a closer look.

Community Property States *vs.* Equitable Distribution States

If you live in Arizona, California, Idaho, Louisiana, Nevada, New Mexico, Texas, Washington, or Wisconsin, you live in a "community property" state. In Alaska, spouses can opt in to the community property system by signing an agreement designating specific assets as community property.

In a *community property state*, the spouses are deemed to equally own all income and assets earned or acquired during the marriage. It doesn't matter who earned the money to buy the house or the plasma television. If it is acquired during the marriage it is owned 50/50 between the spouses. Equal ownership also applies to debts. This means both spouses are equally liable for debts no matter which spouse incurred it.

If you live in one of the other forty-one states you live in an *equitable distribution* state in which property acquired during the marriage belongs to the spouse who earned it. But regardless of who owns it, in a divorce proceeding the property will be divided between the spouses in what the courts consider a "fair and equitable" manner. I talk more about this in a moment, but first we need to cover the difference between separate and marital property.

Separate Property

In most states, property that was yours before the marriage is considered to be separate property and should remain yours.

Items typically considered *separate* property—i.e., owned by you alone and not subject to split:

- 💰 Items that you owned prior to the marriage

- An inheritance received solely by you

- A gift you received solely from a third party

- The pain and suffering portion of a personal injury judgment

- Your engagement ring (because it was given before the marriage)

Marital Property

If it isn't separate property, it is marital and subject to split between the parties including:

- Your wedding band

- Gifts you received during the marriage for birthdays, anniversaries, etc.

- Everything else acquired during the marriage
  - All investments, IRAs, and variable annuities
  - Pension plans—the part earned during the marriage
  - Personal property
  - Real estate
  - Frequent flyer miles
  - Executive compensation, deferred compensation, stock and stock option plans
  - Cash value life insurance

Separate Property Can Become Marital Property!

Unfortunately, there are some situations where assets that were clearly owned by one party prior to marriage are not considered 100-percent separate property. An example is if an asset is comingled with marital property or if it has appreciated during the marriage due to the non-owner spouse's contribution.

It is so easy to accidently take funds that are yours alone and inadvertently reclassify them as jointly owned with your spouse. For example, if you added your spouse as co-owner of your previously owned home or took Aunt Tootie's inheritance and placed it in your joint bank account, then you have probably created a marital asset.

Similarly, if you used inheritance funds to buy a jointly owned vacation home, boat, or other asset, expect the court to consider that a marital asset.

Lastly, don't assume that just because you owned property prior to marriage, no portion of it will be deemed marital property. Judges have wide latitude to divide property in whatever way they feel is fair and equitable.

Appreciation of Separate Assets During the Marriage

This is a state-by-state issue and can be complicated. Many states consider asset appreciation that occurs during the marriage to be marital property. Others will make a determination based on whether the non-owner spouse made a direct or indirect contribution to the growth of the asset.

For example, if the home you owned before marriage increases in value during the marriage as a result of your and your spouse's efforts to maintain and improve it, your spouse may be entitled to a portion of that increase in value.

Likewise, if your business or professional practice increases in value throughout the marriage due in part to your spouse's contributions, your spouse may be entitled to a share of the increase in value upon divorce or your death. By helping entertain clients or staying home with children, it is possible for a spouse to be considered participating in the appreciation of a business and, therefore, entitled to some of the additional value accrued during the marriage.

What Does a "Fair and Equitable" Split Mean?

Many people are surprised to discover that in most states there is no set rule for determining who receives what or how much of the marital property. Having said that, all states now have some form of "no fault" divorce so it is increasingly rare for judges to approve a lopsided division of property based on who is to blame for ending the marriage.

In determining what is fair and equitable, a court will consider a variety of factors. Each state has its own guidelines. For example, in the state of Rhode Island, judges are bound by these considerations in determining property splits:[12]

- 💰 The duration of the marriage

- 💰 The conduct of the parties during the marriage

---

12   General Laws of Rhode Island—Title 15 , Chapter 15-5-16.1

- The contribution of each of the parties during the marriage in the acquisition, preservation, or appreciation in value of their respective estates

- The contribution and services of either party as a homemaker

- The health and age of the parties

- The amount and sources of income of each of the parties

- The occupation and employability of each of the parties

- The opportunity of each party for future acquisition of capital assets and income

- The contribution by one party to the education, training, licensure, business, or increased earning power of the other

- The need of the custodial parent to occupy or own the marital residence and to use or own its household effects taking into account the best interests of the children of the marriage

- Either party's wasteful dissipation of assets or any transfer or encumbrance of assets made in contemplation of divorce without fair consideration

- Any factor which the court shall expressly find to be just and proper.

That last one deserves particular attention. Judges have wide latitude in deciding what is fair and equitable. A good attorney will know how your assigned judge is likely to view your settlement and help you structure it accordingly.

Determining the Value of Your Assets

Once you have identified your marital assets you will need to figure out what they are worth. You need two pieces of information: the valuation date and the value of the assets on that date.

Know Your State's 'Valuation Dates'

One would hope that figuring out the value of your assets would be straightforward. Well, it often isn't.

First off, the value of an asset can vary greatly depending on the "valuation date" chosen, especially with volatile investments such as publicly traded securities. The shares of a single stock can move several percent in a day.

Each state has its own specific rules on what date asset values are locked in. Some states use the date the divorce petition is filed, others the date of separation, and still others the date the divorce is final or the trial date.

There are also different dates assigned depending on whether the asset is considered active or passive. Active assets appreciate based on the actions of the owner, like a business. Passive assets appreciate due to changes in the market, like a publicly traded security. And, to make matters more complex, some assets like rental properties can be considered both active and passive. It can get messy.

Since there is often a considerable delay between separation and your final divorce decree you will want to consult closely with your divorce team to understand your state's rules and, if possible, use a valuation date that is most advantageous to you.

Assigning a Value

Once you know the valuation date you still need to do the research to determine what the value of that asset is as of the date.

For most investment assets it is simply a matter of asking the firm that holds the asset to give you a valuation. For others it can be a bit more complicated.

- Investment accounts can usually be valued by the firm holding them.

- Employer retirement plans such as a 401(k) can be valued by the employer's plan provider. This also applies to executive compensation and other savings plans.

- Pensions will require an actuary or CDFA™ to calculate a value.[13]

- Homes need to be appraised from a qualified real estate professional.

- Businesses need to have business valuation specialist, often a CPA, determine how much it is worth. More on this can be found in Chapter 20.

- Fine art and jewelry require specialized valuations from experts in the field.

- Stock option programs require advanced analysis (discussed in chapter 18).

---

13   More on pension plan valuation can be found in chapter 17. If you have a pension in your household, you will want to read it!

Often there is a negotiation between the spouses to determine the best way to get a fair valuation on high-value assets such as a business or real estate.

Marital Debt

Over the course of a marriage, you may have accumulated not only assets but a number of debts (liabilities) in the form of a mortgage, credit cards, and other types of loans.

It is paramount that decisions be made as to how those debts will be paid off or maintained after the divorce is final.

What Is Considered a Marital Debt?

In non-community property states a person is legally responsible for paying only the debts they alone incurred during the marriage. However, the court will take into account the total debt incurred during the marriage when dividing up property, so it is possible to still pay indirectly for debts your spouse incurred.

Both spouses, however, are generally responsible for debts that relate to their children's education and their food, clothing, shelter, and medical care. And, if debts are registered in joint name, you are both on the hook to pay.

In community property states all debts and assets acquired during the marriage are joint, and both spouses are liable for all debts incurred by the other. In equitable distributions states all debts acquired during the marriage are subject to division between spouses.

Debts incurred after the date of separation are usually the responsibility of the spouse who incurred them. Education debts for children are exempt from this rule. And in general a spouse is not responsible for debts incurred before marriage or after the divorce is final.

Dividing Up Debt in Your Settlement

While most of the focus in divorce finance is on dividing up assets, it is just as important to figure out how to divide up money you owe.

There are three basic ways to divide up debt in your settlement agreement.

- One spouse can agree to pay the bulk of the debts, and an offsetting increase in alimony or marital assets can be given.

- You and your spouse can divide joint property equally and debts equally.

- You and your spouse can liquidate joint property and use the proceeds to pay off marital debts.

Please note that the first two options do not let you out of a legal obligation to pay creditors, even if your spouse will be writing the check. *Vigilance in making sure the debts get paid on time is essential* in protecting your credit rating.

Where possible, I highly recommend paying off debts as you exit your marriage so that you can start your new life with a clean credit record and reduced involvement with your ex on financial issues. But I understand this is simply not feasible for many divorcing couples.

Factors a Judge May Consider

If your case ends up going before a judge (instead of being decided through a mediated agreement), he or she may consider these factors in deciding who is responsible for paying debts:

- Debt from "family" expenses, as described above—clothes, vacations, groceries, and so on—will likely be split between the spouses.

- If the debt was incurred by either husband or wife for his and her own personal use or agenda, then the debt is more likely to be assigned to the person who incurred the debt. Gambling debts and debts incurred to support an affair are likely to be assigned to the person who incurred them.

- The person who will own the asset once the divorce is final is more likely to be assigned the debt, e.g., cars, boats, and "man cave" flat-screen TVs.

Creditors Don't Care about Your Divorce Agreement!

You must understand that creditors do not care about what your divorce agreement says about who will pay the debt. They have a legal right to collect from both of you in the case of a joint debt, or just from the person whose name is on the debt.

So you may be faced with paying a debt even though your ex told you he or she would pay it as part of your agreement. Your best course of action may be to protect your credit rating and seek reimbursement from your ex after the fact.

Actions to Take Now

- Identify all assets and debts acquired during the marriage and, separately, those that were acquired prior to the marriage.

- Make a determination, based on the laws of your state and in consultation with your CDFA™ and attorney, as to what is considered marital and separate property.

- Make note of those assets that are not easily classified due to comingling or other factors.

- Learn about your state's rules on valuation dates and determine whom to contact to get valuations as of those dates.

- If you are working with a divorce financial coach they can highlight the assets that may need further analysis to determine whether they are marital property. They can also prepare for you a concise summary of your assets, both marital and non-marital, for review by your attorney or your mediator, and calculate their true after tax value. Lastly they can develop with you ways to divide assets which support your long range goals and vision.

But first we need to take a close look at all this information and determine your financial strengths and weaknesses.

CHAPTER 9

Taking a Critical Look At Your Finances

"You know why divorces are so expensive?
Because they're worth it!"
—Henny Youngman

J eff is a friend of mine, and we talk a lot. And one of the things good friends do is let each other know when they sense the BS meter going into the yellow zone. With a quick glance our eyes say, "Seriously, bro? Let's get real here." And then the actual story comes out.

This chapter is about getting real with your finances: the good, the bad, and the ugly. After that, we'll create a negotiation strategy and recovery plan so you can get in the best financial position possible to achieve your post-divorce vision.

I should be clear: almost everyone going through divorce has issues with personal finances. Too little cash, underfunded retirements, underwater real estate, credit card debt…it goes on.

Your job is to take an unemotional view of your personal finances and use it to your advantage as you go through your divorce proceedings. Why? One simple reason:

If you know what you need most,
you are more likely to ask for it and get it!

Many financial agreements look great on paper but fail in execution because they do not address one of the spouse's critical needs. If you know what is most important, you will have a better chance of incorporating it into your settlement.

The Four Rules of Financial Security

Personal finance is complicated. But when you get down to it, there are only four rules to follow to set you up for a lifetime of financial security.

Live Within Your Means
It is really important, critically important, to end up with enough income to cover your expenses. That is why you need a crystal-clear idea as to what your expenses will be after divorce.

Have Your Net Worth Spread Across a Mix of Financial Assets
You will want cash for living expenses and your emergency fund, investment assets for your long-term needs like retirement, and perhaps real estate to

live in. The more asset types you own, the better you will be able to ride out the ups and downs of the economy, the stock market, and your work life.

Have Access to Credit

While it is admirable and ideal to live life on cash and have no debt at all, you will want to have the ability to borrow money if necessary. It gives you flexibility and peace of mind. This requires a good credit rating and regular income. See Rule Four!

Keep Debt Under Control

It doesn't matter whether you are the US Government, a corporation, or a person; too much debt can be destructive to your financial health. Whether it is credit cards, student loans, or a mortgage if the balance is too high, you will have trouble meeting your daily expenses. Like salt in a soup…a little makes it delicious, too much and you have a big problem!

Assessing Your Financial Strengths and Weaknesses

So how do your finances look in the context of your divorce? Below are twenty-two questions to ask yourself to help you assess your financial health. Keep in mind some of these may require the assistance of an outside advisor, such as a CPA or CDFA™.

Cash Reserve

- Do I have six months of living expenses in the form of cash?

- Do I have access to non-retirement investments that could be sold if I needed to create cash?

Income

- 💰 Am I employed?

- 💰 Is my take-home pay sufficient to cover my anticipated expenses?

- 💰 If I am not working, will I be able to find work given my current skill set?

- 💰 Does my spouse have a large enough income to pay both child support and alimony so I can get back on my feet?

Investments

- 💰 Do I have funds saved for retirement? Am I on track?

- 💰 Do I have any funds saved for my children's education? Am I on track?

- 💰 Do I or my spouse contribute to a 401(k), pension, or other retirement plan?

Credit

- 💰 Do I have a credit card in my name?

- 💰 Do I have a credit history?

- 💰 Is my credit rating above 700?

Debt/Loans

- 💰 Is my total mortgage/home equity debt less than the value of my home(s)?

- 💰 Am I able to pay off my total credit card balance every month?

💰 Do I have outstanding auto loans for the car I drive? Is the loan in my name?

Business Interests

💰 Does the business represent the majority of my family's net worth?

💰 Has the business been valued recently by a qualified professional?

💰 Are there other partners involved in the business?

Your Home

💰 Is my home in good shape, especially the roof and heating system?

💰 If I wanted to sell it, is it in a condition where I could get full market price?

Budget

💰 Do I know how much it will cost me to live as a single person after my divorce?

💰 Can I afford the maintenance costs of my marital home if I wish to stay there?

Once you have answered the above questions look at the "no's" and decide what it means to your negotiation game plan.

For instance, if you answered "no" to the question of being able to afford the maintenance of your home, yet you still want to live there, you will need to have additional income in the form of a higher paying job or alimony.

Similarly, if most of your family's assets are locked up in the "bricks and mortar" of a business, you will need to establish a value for the business and find ways to pay out in a lump sum, installments, or as an ongoing income stream the value due the non-owner spouse.

Identifying Your "Must Haves" vs. "Like to Haves"

I can't stress enough the importance of going into negotiations with clarity about what is most important to your financial happiness. You simply need to know your priorities.

As an example, if living in the marital home is absolutely essential it is likely you will need to take on a certain amount of maintenance expense and perhaps reduce some discretionary spending. If you want to rent for a while and purchase your own home at some point, you may need to build up your credit and income in order to qualify for a mortgage.

Everything is connected in divorce finance, and it is likely that once you put a stake into the ground as to what is most important to you, other parts of your settlement will adjust to accommodate it. In general, in a no-fault divorce you can't have everything you desire and will need to make compromises, especially if income or assets are limited. But if you have a clear view of your "must haves," your compromises will be the ones right for you.

Below are some of the things people often list as "must haves" and "like to haves." Remember, though, that this is a personal decision.

Sample "Must Haves"

- A safe and comfortable place to live for you and your children
- Income to support the daily needs of your household
- Time or training to establish a work life, if necessary
- Positive cash flow so you don't need to take on debt
- Keep the family business
- Close connection with your children
- The least disruption and upheaval for your children
- A balance of assets from the marital property
  + Cash, retirement, college funding
- To stay in the marital home

Sample "Like to Haves"

- Live in a certain part of the country
- Be able to maintain work/life balance
- Maintain your present lifestyle
- Money to buy nice things, take vacations, etc…
- To not have to work for an extended period of time, or ever
- Keep personal belongings that have sentimental value

These are just suggestions to help you differentiate between the two categories. Your "must haves" are totally valid simply because they are yours.

Creating the Financial Information Package

If you retain a financial coach, he or she should prepare for you a financial information package for your attorney or mediator (or both).

This goes beyond the required court financial disclosure forms and serves as the basis for creating a negotiation game plan. It contains not only the data but (optionally) potential asset divisions and projections showing how your net worth and income will change over time.

Examples of these reports can be found at http://www.familylaw software.com/reports.html.[14]

Actions to Take Now

Using the worksheets found in the back of this book, or in the free financial planner you have downloaded from our website,

- Take a critical look at your finances and assess your strengths and weaknesses. Write down your assessments on the strengths and weaknesses worksheet at the back of this book, or in the implementation guide.

- Review the list above and write down your "must haves" and "like to haves" on the worksheet provided. The downloadable implementation guide has bonus content in the form of 29 additional questions which will help you develop a game plan for negotiations.

---

14   There are a number of divorce financial planning software tools available. We use Family Law Software because it is the industry standard and exceptionally powerful.

- 💰 Meet with your financial coach if you have one and review your worksheets.

- 💰 Get the Financial Information Package (FIP) from your financial coach once he or she has prepared it for you.

- 💰 Schedule a meeting with your attorney or mediator to review the FIP. Your financial coach might be helpful at this meeting.

- 💰 If you do not have a coach, organize your information for a meeting with your attorney or mediator to discuss your negotiation game plan.

STAGE 2

Negotiating An Agreement Right For You

CHAPTER 10

Creating Your Personal Negotiation Game Plan

"I'm not upset about my divorce.
I'm only upset I'm not a widow."
—Roseanne Barr

I hate chess. I grew up with an older brother who was a whiz at everything academic. He spent countless hours playing chess and conjugating Latin verbs while I watched *The Jetsons* and avoided my homework. So it is odd that I am the one writing about how to create a game plan for divorce negotiations and am the big financial strategist. He only became a doctor.

So now that you have solidified your vision for the future and know the strengths and weaknesses of your personal finances, it is time to make a plan for entering divorce negotiations.

Here is the formula for creating a game plan:

Vision + Strengths and Weaknesses + Must Haves = Game Plan

Your game plan is based upon what you want long term (your vision), the realities of your financial situation (strengths and weaknesses), and your most critical priorities (must haves).

If you are using a divorce financial coach, he or she will have prepared this list for you based on an analysis of your situation and your conversations, and will have organized your data so that it is clear and easy to understand.

Meeting with Your Attorney

In a litigated divorce you will want to meet with your attorney and give him or her a copy of your Financial Information Package.

If you are working with a financial coach the Financial Information Package will contain the analyses he or she prepared for you: an asset summary, your strengths and weaknesses summary, and a lifestyle analysis. He or she will also have made a note of any special issues. If you are working on your own, it will contain the worksheets you have filled out as you went through your preparation and your required financial affidavit.

You hired your attorney to advocate for you in court, and negotiate on your behalf. Your goal should be to make it crystal clear what you need most in your settlement based on your vision and "must haves" so they can create appropriate proposals for consideration.

You should also share with your attorney any settlement ideas you have developed with a financial coach that you would find acceptable. Attorneys should find this valuable, as it will give them a blueprint with which to begin negotiations with the other side.

Your attorney may have other ideas he or she would like to see tested as alternatives to the ones you have provided. A divorce financial analyst can easily create powerful projections for you that will help you see how these alternatives support your long term net worth and cash flow. A simple net-worth and cash-flow chart can tell a powerful story and make it easy to judge whether a settlement is fair and equitable, or potentially disastrous.[15]

Meeting with Your Mediator

If you choose to mediate, take with you to the initial meeting three pages of information: your vision page, your strengths and weaknesses page and your "must haves." Mediators will often schedule this meeting as a one-on-one session with you to get a general idea about what you are looking for in your overall agreement and address any concerns you may have about the mediation process.

You should expect that your mediator will approach building your agreement in steps, perhaps starting with the child sharing and parenting plan, and then moving into financial issues. Mediators should share with you their methodology for ensuring all issues are addressed.

---

15   Samples of these charts can be found at the Family Law website. http://www.family lawsoftware.com/reports.html.

The Role of a Financial Coach

The financial expert is becoming more and more accepted as an essential part of your advisor team.

In a Mediation

Ask your mediator how your financial coach should be involved, if you have one. If your coach is working strictly on your behalf, versus with you and your spouse as a couple, it is likely the mediator would prefer the coach not to attend meetings and instead help you between mediation sessions make, create, and evaluate financial proposals.

If your financial coach is working with you as a couple, your mediator may be comfortable having your coach sit in on the sessions dealing with financial issues.

In a Litigated Divorce

Your financial coach is part of your divorce team and should be used in any way that can be helpful to the financial aspects of your settlement, including but not limited to analyzing the long-term benefits of various proposals, putting your final financial settlement in easy-to-understand summaries for your approval, and preparing settlement information for review by the judge.[16]

---

16   In our work we routinely sit in on negotiation meetings with our clients and their attorneys to add clarity to the morass of numbers surrounding their divorce. Whether it is to determine a sensible counteroffer, or compare alternative proposals we are often there at the table with our laptop creating on the spot illustrations that can move the conversation forward.

What Does a Successful Financial Negotiation Look Like?

In the eyes of the court, your agreement needs to pass the fair and equitable test. That does not mean assets are split exactly 50/50 as there are many factors judges must consider. He or she typically will be looking at what is best for the welfare of any children first and the needs of the parents second.

Other tests of fairness include the ability for the nonworking or lower wage spouse to gain self-sufficiency over time and whether the asset division is balanced given the specifics of your divorce.

But from your vantage point, for your negotiations to be considered successful your settlement should give you at a minimum your "must haves," and your long-term vision should be supported within the limitations of your family finances.

I talk more about how to develop and refine your settlement in chapter 21.

Actions to Take Now

- Schedule a meeting with your attorney or mediator and share with him or her the financial information package prepared by you or your financial coach.

- Discuss your priorities with your attorney and agree on an initial negotiation strategy. You would not typically have this with your mediator.

Coming Up:
Essential Knowledge

Five Tests Every Divorce Settlement Must Pass

Considerations in Keeping the Marital Home

Child Support

Spousal Support/Alimony

Divorce and Taxes

Social Security and Divorce

Retirement Assets

Executive Compensation &
Non-Qualified Compensation Plans

Guaranteeing Your Settlement with Life Insurance

Dealing with Business Interests

Refining and Finalizing Your Agreement

CHAPTER 11

Five Tests Every Divorce Settlement Must Pass

"They say marriages are made in heaven
But so is thunder and lightning."
—*Clint Eastwood*

*L*et's skip a few steps and put you in the mind-set of having created an agreement. So after weeks and months of negotiation, sleepless nights, and too much Pepto-Bismol you have finally come up with a divorce agreement you are happy with.

After all, you got the house, more than half the assets, and the antique dining room furniture that makes you feel like you are in Paris at dinnertime. You are ready to sign on the dotted line and get on with your life. But is it really a good settlement for you? Here are five tests every good divorce settlement must pass.

It Is Based on Economic Reality

Family finances are not simple. Some expenses are easily identified like the mortgage and the cable bill, but many others are not—the kids' allowances and your eight-dollar daily lunches. And projecting the budgets for two separate households adds more complexity. So it is imperative that the data on which you are basing your agreement reflects your actual financial life.

As discussed in chapter 7, I recommend my clients take a year's worth of *all* expenses and categorize each one so they can get a clear picture of where their money goes, and then assume those expenses grow each year by 5 percent. A cash flow analysis is very helpful in projecting into the future how each household would fare under a proposed settlement.

Other numbers that need to pass the reality test are growth assumptions for your investment and retirement accounts, and for inflation. A major flaw of most divorce financial planning tools is that they use long-term averages to predict the future value of securities as if you get that return consistently every year. Unfortunately, markets do not work that way, so your projections could be an overly rosy view of your financial future. Keep estimates conservative and you will be well served.

Your 50 Percent Is the Right 50 Percent

If you have gone through the exercise of establishing your vision, defining your strengths and weaknesses, and determining your "must haves," you should be in a position to negotiate an agreement that helps get you what you need most.

Dividing up marital assets is not the same as taking a cake and simply cutting down the middle. That is because your family's net worth is really made up of a lot of different things, from real estate to checking accounts to your living room furniture. You can't sit on a checking account, and you can't buy groceries with the family heirloom, so you need to make sure the assets you end up with are the ones that support your specific needs.

As an example, if your agreement gives you the family home in exchange for 401(k) or savings accounts, you may find yourself with too small of a cash reserve for paying unexpected bills and maintaining the property.

If you have excellent cash flow from work or other sources, this may not be an issue. But in the end, you want your agreement to provide adequate and reliable income to pay your bills, access to a cash reserve for emergencies, a place to live that you can afford, and assets set aside for your retirement and education expenses.

Assets Are Valued Accurately

When your financial life is laid out on a piece of paper it has the appearance of accuracy. In my experience some of those numbers are guesses at best, and others are downright misleading.

One common mistake is not adjusting the value of 401(k) and retirement accounts to account for taxes due at withdrawal, which can lower their real value by up to 40 percent. I have a chapter on that coming up.

Other heavily taxed assets that may be overvalued are stock options and deferred compensation plans. Pension plans, because of their complexity, require special analysis so they are fairly valued both in today's dollars and as a future income stream. Lastly, home and business market values need to be properly appraised by trained professionals.

Spousal and Child-Support Commitments Are Insured

If your settlement has significant income commitments in the form of child or spousal support, it ideally should be backed by an insurance policy on the life of the payer. A simple term insurance policy owned by the person receiving the income is a way of making sure you have the financial support you are counting on. This is discussed in detail in chapter 19.

It Passes the Stress Test

Despite the care and attention some agreements are given to "get the numbers right," I have to concede that there is a lot of estimating going on. So it pays to "stress test" your agreement to see if it still passes muster if things go wrong.

A stress test begins by adjusting a few core assumptions beginning with how your expenses and assets will grow over time.

If your expenses grow twice as fast as you expect, and your investments earn half as much, what is the resulting long-term impact on your finances? If you suffer a setback through job loss or an unexpected expense, will your settlement give you the resources to deal with it?

So now that we have an idea of some tests your agreement must pass, let us look at the most common financial elements of divorce agreements and how you might handle them.

CHAPTER 12

Considerations in Keeping the Marital Home

"I am a marvelous housekeeper.
Every time I leave a man I keep his house!"
—Zsa Zsa Gabor

My wife and I moved into our home in Rhode Island in 1993. I moved out in 2003.

I was completely attached to that very ordinary house. The funky yard I mowed, the fireplace where we gathered, and the kitchen where I made pasta by hand all seemed irreplaceable. Leaving was hard. Then my kids would show up at my little rental home and we would cook together, and eat all crammed into our little kitchen and it would all be okay. My kids talk fondly about those early days now, but at the time it was quite a difficult life change.

It is understandable, and common practice among divorcing couples, to try to keep the marital home. Whether it is to keep stability in the lives of children or because there are emotional connections to the property, holding onto the marital home is often proposed in many property settlements.

Here are some considerations to ponder to help you make a decision that is right for you.

Why You May Want to Keep the Home

The Children May Benefit

Children in general are better able to withstand the stresses of divorcing parents if they have environmental stability. Studies show that children who remain in the same house, the same school, and the same social network do better than those who are moved out of familiar surroundings.

Staying in the family home, though, is only one of several factors affecting a child's post-divorce adjustment. The child's age, temperament, level of parental contact and, most importantly, the intensity of conflict between parents, also affect their mental well-being.

You May Need Time to Build Income and Credit

If you don't have a credit history, or are just getting back into the workforce, it may not be possible to downsize and purchase another property because you may not qualify for a mortgage. And, if income is mainly through child support or alimony, it may take six months to a year of payments before a lender will approve your loan. A mortgage broker can tell you whether you or your spouse will have a problem getting a new mortgage.

It Costs Money to Move

Between appraisals, agent's commissions, and moving costs, not to mention any required improvements to prepare the home for sale, a lot of money can be spent going from one residence to another. If cash is tight, or you are forced to go into debt to prepare your home for sale, you may find it easier to hold on to the property for the time being.

It May Be a Bad Time to Sell

Real estate values, like other investments, are cyclical. There are times when they are appreciating and times when they are depreciating. If your home is worth less than when it was first purchased, or you owe more than its current value, it may be reasonable to hold off on the sale until prices recover. Of course, if you are staying in the same local market, what you buy may also be more expensive. A real estate professional can help you assess your home's value and trends in the local marketplace.

The Cost of a Mortgage May Be Higher

Another consideration is the cost of money, i.e., your mortgage interest rate. If you have a super low interest rate on your mortgage, it is possible a new mortgage of the same amount will cost you considerably more. A mortgage broker can tell you what price home you can afford based on your income and prevailing interest rates.

Why You May Want to Sell the Home

You May Not Be Able to Afford It

Homes cost money…sometimes lots of it. The cost of a home goes beyond the mortgage. You need to consider property taxes, insurance, and upkeep. A new roof or heating system can cost thousands to replace, lawns need to be mowed, and driveways repaired.

Moving to a simpler and less expensive property, or even renting for a period of time, may be financially desirable if it means you no longer run up your credit card balance and can save for retirement and your children's education.

You May Have Too Much of Your Net Worth Tied Up

If your intention is to own your marital residence in your name alone, you may need to give your spouse more assets such as cash and retirement accounts. As a result, it is possible to end up with most of your net worth in the bricks and mortar of your home, but little in cash for living expenses, emergencies, or retirement savings.

Managing the Home in Your Settlement

Sell Outright and Split the Proceeds

If your home value has appreciated since its purchase, you may have significant equity in your home. By selling the property you and your ex-spouse would be able to use your home sale profits to settle your debts and each make a fresh financial start.

Usually, one spouse remains in the house until it sells, and both parties agree to split the costs of preparing the house for sale. Once a buyer is found and the house is sold, generally the parties will split the proceeds of the sale after deducting all closing costs, property taxes, and agent commissions.

One Spouse Buys Out the Other and Owns the Home

If one spouse wants to stay in the marital home and own it outright, the title needs to change from joint name to the name of the spouse residing in the house, and the non-owner spouse receives his or her equity in the home either upfront or over time. There are three ways this is typically accomplished:

The Non-Resident Spouse is Given Other Assets

The other spouse receives assets in place of equity in the home (assuming they are available). These may be retirement or investment accounts or other property.

The House Is Refinanced

Since most jointly owned property is supported by a mortgage also in joint name, the real estate mortgage usually has to be refinanced to remove the other spouse's name. As part of that refinancing, the spouse that is awarded the real estate takes on a larger mortgage using the additional funds to pay off the other spouse's interest.

A Payment Plan Is Established

A spouse's interest may also be paid out over time, with or without interest, as negotiated between the parties. This approach is usually only used when there are no other assets that can be used to equalize the property division. The payoff amount and period may depend on the respective incomes of the parties.

Joint Ownership with One Spouse Living There

Some couples may be comfortable owning the home jointly for a period of time after the divorce, perhaps until children graduate from school or the custodial spouse is able to improve his or her financial position. Only one spouse lives in the property but the home is owned and financed in both names.

There is ordinarily a written agreement that specifies the conditions under which this arrangement will function. It may contain language allowing residence "until the minor children reach the age of eighteen," with the home to be sold and equity divided at a later date. Sometimes there are additional contingencies, such as a provision that the agreement ends if the spouse who remains in the home remarries or cohabitates.

Lawyers advise that any such agreement make clear how the equity is to be calculated and divided when the home is ultimately sold. It should also make clear how the costs of house payments, taxes, repairs, and maintenance of the home are to be split between the owners, and what will happen if those responsibilities aren't met.

Actions to Take Now

The decision to keep or sell a home is a complicated and often an emotional one. You will want to:

- Consult real estate specialists who can help you determine the market value of your home and the real estate market,

- Contact a CPA to evaluate the tax implications of selling your property and a mortgage broker to see whether a new mortgage can be acquired, and

- You may want to consult a child development specialist to determine what is best for your children's emotional health. Take enough time to make a fully informed and reasoned decision.

- If you are working with a financial coach they can show you how your long-term net worth and cash flow is affected based on your assumed home expenses. They can also help you work through credit or refinancing issues by connecting you with reputable mortgage professionals.

Personal Note

I moved three times after that first rental home. Along the way I became engaged, bought a house, became un-engaged, and moved to a two-family duplex. Three years later I bought a home on the other side of town where I live now. We kept the family home for a period of time, but my ex eventually got a place of her own. And the kids are doing fine.

From my personal experience, and the experiences of my clients, my observation is that children are surprisingly adaptable. The more respectful and cordial parents are with one another the better off the children will be.

You should take comfort in knowing that after all the twists and turns, things eventually smooth out and new memories are made.

CHAPTER 13

Child Support

"There can be no keener revelation of a society's soul
than the way in which it treats its children."
—Nelson Mandela

In our neighborhood in Connecticut, we were surrounded by mostly old Yankee families with names like Cox, Voight, and Baldwin. But there we were, the family with the long Sicilian name no one could pronounce. We shared our Mediterranean heritage with one other family, the Defeoes, down at the bottom of the hill. They had seven kids and were always the go-to house for fun.

As long as you stayed out of Mrs. Defeo's way a good time could be had. Despite the fear she could instill, each one those kids got the support and attention they needed to become confident and successful adults. I write this chapter with Mrs. Defeo, and all caring parents, in mind.

Nothing creates more confusion and anxiety than the possibility of paying or receiving income in the form of spousal support (alimony) and child support. These money transfers can make or break the financial life of either spouse if they are not implemented fairly in a divorce settlement.

In this chapter we explore child support—how it works, the various formulas in use around the country, and what you need to know going into your negotiations.

Child Support Basics

The family court system of your state has, above all else, a responsibility to make sure the children of divorcing couples do not suffer needless financial and emotional harm. Therefore, child support payments from one parent to the other, or some other way of ensuring the children's financial needs are met, are required for a settlement to be approved.

This is not to say that all settlements must have child support payments. If children spend equal time with each parent, and if the parents' incomes are nearly identical, the court could approve a settlement without child support payments. But this is more the exception than the rule.

Some Criticisms

Child support formulas are all flawed in some way. For example, virtually every state requires one parent to pay the other rather than paying for children's expenses out of a jointly funded account. And in all states one parent must be designated as the custodial parent even where time is split evenly between households.

Despite these flaws, state courts are obligated under federal law to have statutes and processes that protect the needs of children. So they stick with their chosen formula as a way to create consistency, protect children, and give parents the opportunity to use the court to advocate for changes to their child support obligations. It is an imperfect system but a necessary one.

Child Support Models

You will find that each state subscribes to one of three approaches to calculating child support.

The *Income Shares Model* is the most popular approach in use today. It is based on the concept that the child should receive the same proportion of parental income that he or she would have received if the parents lived together. It allocates an amount of support for the child using a percentage formula based on the parents' pooled or combined income.

The philosophy behind it is that the parents' income after divorce should still be looked at as one income pool and spent for the benefit of all household members, including any children.

The *Melson Formula* builds on the concept of the Income Shares Model but takes it a step closer toward economic reality by first deducting the parents' basic living expenses from each of their respective incomes.

It is considered by advocates to be a fairer way to determine child support. It is only in use in Delaware, Hawaii, and Montana.

The *Percentage of Income Model* sets support as a percentage of *only the noncustodial parent's income*; the custodial parent's income is not considered.

This model has two variations: the Flat Percentage Model, where a fixed percentage of income is paid regardless of the amount of income earned, and the Varying Percentage Model, which reduces the percentage set aside for child support payments as income increases. It is in use by ten states today.

Six Things to Know about Child Support

Child support guidelines vary by state, but here are some general rules:

- Child support is considered more important than spousal support (alimony) in the eyes of the courts. The children's welfare comes first…spouse's second.

- Child support payments vary by state. You need to look at the formula your state uses. Every state has an online calculator to determine what is likely to be paid.

- Under the Income Shares Model, the relative income of each parent and which parent is designated as the custodial parent are the major factors in calculating child support. But other factors may be considered, such as:
    - Whether there are existing child support obligations from a previous marriage
    - Which parent is paying for health insurance and day care costs
    - Extraordinary medical costs for the parent or child
    - Additional nights spent at the noncustodial parent's home, i.e., parenting credit.

- What one considers "income" varies considerably by state. It could be gross income, net income, imputed income, or some other form. Bonuses and investment income may or may not be considered.

- Child support may be raised upward or downward from the state guidelines based on any number of factors such as unique needs of the children, other expenses being picked up by the paying parent (like private school), and whether the calculated payment is much more than is needed.

- Child support eventually ends, typically at the age of majority, which is age eighteen in most states. Some states allow payments to continue if the child is attending college. Check your state's guidelines and statutes to see if this applies to you.

Child support guidelines vary greatly by state. You should consult with an attorney to discuss how the courts are likely to view and calculate the payment of child support based on your unique circumstances.

Actions to Take

- Look online at your state's child support guidelines and find out what type of formula they use.

- Run the child support calculator.

- If you are working with a financial coach they can run cash flow projections to show you how the receipt or payment of child support would affect your overall income, savings, and net assets over time. They can also show you how alternatives to child support, such as additional property or spousal support, may be beneficial to you and your family.

CHAPTER 14

Spousal Support (Alimony)

*"Some people ask the secret of our long marriage. We take time to
go to a restaurant two times a week. A little candlelight, dinner,
soft music, and dancing. She goes Tuesdays, I go Fridays."*
—Henry Youngman

P lease excuse the image above. It is meant to show how much has
changed since the early days of alimony when many comics used
it as grist for their stand-up routines, portraying it as an unfair giveaway
from an ex-husband to an undeserving ex-wife.

The fact is that alimony—or spousal support, as it is more aptly
called—is a necessary part of many divorces providing the receiving spouse,
man or woman, with a reasonable level of income so as not to be placed
in undue hardship.

There is wide variation as to how alimony is awarded, and in many
states it is a highly subjective decision based on many factors a judge might

consider. But clearly we have moved away from the antiquated view of "free income for life" toward one that is based more on need and fairness.

Alimony

Alimony is a word that has a lot of emotional impact, triggering for some people feelings of anxiety and fear. A better word for it is "spousal support," which more closely aligns with how the courts view it.

Alimony is typically categorized as one of three types: temporary, rehabilitative, and permanent.

Temporary Alimony

Temporary alimony, or alimony "pendente lite," is often awarded during the period the divorce proceeding is pending. If a long pre-divorce separation is anticipated, the court may require alimony payments so the lower income spouse can meet living expenses.

Rehabilitative Alimony

Generally, rehabilitative alimony is used to support the spouse during a period of retraining or re-education for entry into the workforce, thereby enabling the spouse to become self-supporting.

The courts are more compelled to award this type of alimony where the spouse seeking it has some potential for establishing a viable career. There is a trend to treat more alimony awards as "rehabilitative" with an expectation that each spouse will eventually become financially self-sufficient.

Permanent Alimony

Permanent alimony becomes effective once the divorce is final. It can be paid in a variety of ways including lump sum payments, periodic payments, or in-kind payments where services are paid for directly.

Despite the seemingly permanent nature of this type of award, it usually does not last forever (i.e., until the recipient's death). In most jurisdictions there is no prescribed period for alimony payments. However, this appears to be changing as courts have been looking for a way to strike a balance between the needs of the payer spouse and the payee.

10 Things to Know about Alimony

- It varies widely state by state. Look at your state's guidelines.

- It is gender neutral. Either spouse may be required to pay alimony to the other.

- It is not mandatory, and courts have wide latitude to determine whether an alimony payment is warranted based on the specific facts of the case.

- It is generally considered temporary and is designed to allow nonworking or lower income spouses the time needed to gain employment sufficient to support themselves.

- Alimony is last in line after child support and asset splits. Courts typically will make a decision only after child support and the split of marital assets are divided and agreed upon.

💰 Lifetime alimony is becoming less common.

   ✦ Some states, like Massachusetts, have done away with lifetime alimony in favor of a tiered system that limits the duration of payments based on the length of the marriage.[17]

💰 Judges look at many factors in determining whether alimony is warranted including:

   ✦ The earning capacity of the lower earning spouse

   ✦ The placement and custody of children

   ✦ Age and health of the parties

   ✦ The length of the marriage

   ✦ The paying spouse's ability to pay and assets available.

💰 Alimony payments may go up or down over time, or end early based on any number of factors including:

   ✦ Remarriage or cohabitation

   ✦ Death or any significant change in either party's circumstances.

💰 Alimony is considered alimony (vs. child support or property transfer) only if a number of rules are followed, such as living in separate households, payment in cash, and the inclusion of specific language in your agreement that identifies the payments as alimony. There are other rules as well so, again, talk to your accountant.

---

17   For example, for marriages under five years, payments will last 50 percent of the years married; for marriages lasting five to ten years, 60 percent of the years married; for ten to fifteen years 70 percent of the years spent married, and so on.

💰 Alimony should not end at about the time child support payments are scheduled to end, lest the IRS designate them as child support payments in disguise. More on this in a moment.

Alimony Can Be Considered a Property Transfer by the IRS

This is important. Alimony payments **must** be delivered in a way such that they do not have the appearance of being simply property transfers. Read that twice.

Alimony payments are no longer tax deductible by the payer and taxable as income to the payee. In the past, these benefits could be reversed if payments dropped off rapidly in the first three years.

The IRS did not want to give tax benefits to people who were simply transferring property pursuant to a divorce. To prevent this they looked at the alimony payments made in the first three years and ran them through a formula to see if they violated IRS rules.[18]

Your CDFA™ or CPA can help you determine whether an alimony payment plan runs the risk of being re-characterized as a property transfer.

Alimony Can Become Child Support

The IRS requires that alimony be for spousal support, and child support be for the kids. So they came up with a rule, the "Child Contingency Rule," that would reclassify alimony as nondeductible child support if

---

18 The alimony recapture rules can be found on the IRS website at www.irs.gov/publications/p17/ch18.html.

the alimony ends or is reduced within six months of when the child ceases to be a minor.

For example, if your child turned eighteen this August 1st and would no longer be a minor, alimony should not have ended between February 1st of this year (six months prior) and January 31st of next year (six months after).

Also, if alimony was slated to change based on other child-related events (such as the child leaving home, getting married, or becoming employed), the IRS would have nullified the tax deductibility.[19] The reduction in alimony payments made from day one would have been cancelled and reclassified as child support.

What followed was a potentially messy situation as taxes that had been paid by the recipient were refunded, and tax benefits incurred by the payer were paid back to the IRS. As mentioned earlier, the IRS has made alimony payments a tax free transfer so this issue no longer applies to new divorces.

Actions to Take

- Look at your state's alimony laws to get an appreciation for how they treat spousal support.

- Work with your attorney to understand how a court might view alimony in your case. Would it be rehabilitative, temporary, or permanent? What is the justification?

---

19   Events also include the child attaining a specified age or income level, dying, marrying, leaving school, leaving the spouse's household, or gaining employment.

💰 If you are working with a financial coach they can help you determine how best to balance child support, alimony, and property transfers in your settlement.

  * They can model various combinations of alimony, child support, and asset splits so as to maximize after-tax income for both parties.

  * They have special alimony calculation software that can show you how various alimony payment amounts will affect your long-term financial security.

  * They can also flag potential IRS issues that might lead to alimony recapture or re-characterization of alimony as child support.

CHAPTER 15

Divorce and Taxes

"I am proud to be paying taxes in the United States.
The only thing is I could be just as proud for half the money."
—Arthur Godfrey

If I were you, this is one of the last chapters I would want to read. Unless you are an accountant, taxes can be a dry, boring, and mind-numbing subject. But when looked at from the standpoint of their bottom line financial impact in a divorce it is almost interesting reading.

Taxes routinely kill finances in a divorce. They reduce the value of assets you receive in your settlement either not at all or a ridiculous amount and most people, including some divorce professionals, don't adequately account for them.

So I encourage you to read this chapter and get the facts you need. It's not very long, and you will be better off for it.

Property Transfers in Divorce Are Usually Tax-Free

The first thing to know about taxes in divorce is how few there actually are when you move assets between you and your spouse as part of your divorce settlement.

The federal tax code (Section 1041) allows you to divvy up your marital property in whatever way you see fit without triggering a tax liability. That is because you are not selling assets to your spouse in the eyes of the IRS, but merely transferring them as part of a divorce. You are also shifting the original cost of that asset. When the property is eventually sold by the recipient taxes will be due based on the gain and tax rate in effect at that time.

There are very few instances where this rule doesn't apply. As long as both you and your spouse are American citizens you get this deferred taxation. It even applies in the case of a legally recognized common law marriage.[20]

Here is an example. Bill and Margaret bought a rental property 15 years ago for $150,000. It is now worth $300,000 and is transferred as part of their divorce settlement to Margaret. Five years later Margaret sells the property for $350,000 and is responsible for paying taxes on the entire gain of $200,000.[21]

Here is another example. Quentin and Josephine have been good investors and have $75,000 in a stock portfolio for which they initially

---

20   States that recognize common law marriages for divorce settlement purposes include Alabama, Colorado, the District of Columbia, Georgia, Iowa, Kansas, Montana, Ohio, Oklahoma, Pennsylvania, Rhode Island, South Carolina, and Texas. Be sure to consult with an attorney and your tax advisor if you believe you are in a common law marriage.

21   This is a simplified example. The taxable gain would be affected by depreciation and improvements made to the property. And if this were the marital residence the gain would be reduced by the "home sale exclusion" which is discussed later in this chapter.

invested $25,000. Quentin gets the stock portfolio as part of his settlement. He picks up the original cost basis of $25,000 and will pay taxes on any profits over this amount when he sells the securities.

There are a couple of conditions to get this special tax treatment. First, the IRS requires the transfers be "incident to divorce." In general, this means they occurred within one year of the divorce or are in some other way related to the end of the marriage. Any property exchanges that happen after the one year mark is subject to review by the IRS, but if they are part of a formal divorce agreement, they are likely to be covered. In any event, the IRS expects all transfers to be completed within six years of the final divorce decree.

It is important to note that these rules apply to assets that are transferred "as is" and not liquidated. So selling investment assets like stocks and mutual funds and giving the proceeds to your spouse as part of your settlement may trigger a potential tax you would rather live without. The same thing goes for cash withdrawals from most IRA's and retirement accounts.[22, 23]

The rest of this chapter deals with how taxes affect the value of assets that are received as part of your settlement when they are eventually sold after your divorce is final.

Retirement Accounts May be Heavily Taxed

One of the reasons property settlements are often not equitable is that the impact of taxes on retirement accounts is not considered.

---

22   There are times that it may be most appropriate to sell some assets and pay the taxes as part of your overall settlement strategy. But this is the exception, and you will want to speak with your tax advisor before doing so.
23   Roth IRA's allow you to withdraw your original contributions without paying a tax. Gains on those contributions however are taxable.

While employer retirement plans and IRAs are wonderful vehicles for accumulating tax-deferred wealth, they may lose a lot of value to taxes when withdrawn. Any distributions you make are added to your other taxable income and the total is subject to income tax. When you factor in both federal and state tax it is possible to pay as much as 45 percent in tax for every dollar withdrawn. And, if funds are withdrawn before the age of 59½, there is another 10 percent additional tax that may be assessed. There are exceptions to this penalty that can be found on the IRS website.

Certain employer-based retirement accounts such as 401(k)s and pensions are not subject to tax when being divided as part of a divorce property settlement. But the employer must be instructed via a Qualified Domestic Relations Order (QDRO).[24] You will still pay taxes when the assets are withdrawn at retirement.

Home Sweet Home

Unlike retirement accounts, which are taxed from the first dollar withdrawn, your home is a relatively privileged asset.

If, as part of your divorce, you and your ex decide to sell your home, much of your net gain over your purchase price (plus improvements) will not be taxed.

---

24   A QDRO (often called a "quadro") is the document that directs an employer plan to transfer assets to an "alternate payee." Most but not all firms have plans that provide for this type of division. QDRO preparation has become a standard part of the paperwork created once a divorce is finalized. More of this is discussed in the Recovery Stage section of this book.

The rules are somewhat complex but you avoid tax on the first $250,000 of gain on the sale of your primary home if you have owned the home and lived there at least two years out of the last five. Married couples filing jointly can exclude up to $500,000 as long as either one has owned the residence and both used it as a primary home for at least two out of the last five years.

For sales following a divorce, you and your ex can still each exclude up to $250,000 of gain on your individual returns, assuming the ownership and use rules are met. The rules are obviously complicated so consult your tax advisor on your specific situation.

Alimony vs. Child Support—They Are Now Treated the Same

Alimony and child support have until recently been treated differently by the IRS. Alimony had been tax deductible by the payer and taxable to the receiver but changed as a result of the Tax Cuts and Jobs Act of 2018.

While "tax free" sounds attractive for many couples there was a substantial benefit in taking the tax deduction even if the receiving spouse paid taxes on what they received. For payors in the highest tax bracket the tax deduction could lower their cost of alimony by over 40%. For many couples this helped justify paying more support to the receiving spouse.

As was discussed in chapter 14, payments must not be front-loaded in the first three years; otherwise, they risk being considered part of the property settlement. And they must not end within six months of any child turning the age of majority.

Child support is a tax-free transfer of funds between spouses. The payer doesn't get a deduction and the recipient doesn't pay income tax.

Use the Correct Filing Status on Your Tax Return

Your marital status is determined as of the last day of the calendar year. If you are still married on December 31 of the tax year, you can decide to file a joint return, especially if you can amicably deal with your spouse after the divorce. In this scenario, you should also weigh possible tax savings when deciding whether to file jointly or "married filing separately."

Alternatively, if you became divorced on or before December 31, you have the option of filing as a single taxpayer or head of household for that year. For many people, filing as head of household will result in a lower tax obligation.

To qualify for head of household filing status, you must meet numerous requirements. These include having lived apart from your spouse for the last six months of the tax year and paying more than half the cost of keeping the primary residence for your child or other qualifying dependents you claim as a tax exemption.

An accountant or other tax advisor can help you determine what is most advantageous given your circumstances.

Actions to Take

- Become familiar with how taxes will affect the value of the assets in your divorce.

- Speak with an accountant about any complex assets not described in this chapter, such as rental properties or business interests, to learn about their tax treatment.

💰 If you are working with a financial coach have them run the following projections:

+ A "Marital Property Division on an After-Tax Basis" report that will help you determine whether a settlement is fair and equitable

+ A "Projected Net Income after Taxes and Expenses" report.

CHAPTER 16

Social Security and Divorce

*"Down in Washington they're playing with Social Security
like it's some kind of government program!"*
—*George W. Bush*

O ne of the areas of retirement planning frequently overlooked during divorce is Social Security and how benefits may be affected. In short, getting divorced too quickly can mean that the nonworking or low-wage-earning ex-spouse may not be eligible to receive benefits they would otherwise be entitled to.

An Issue for Marriages Lasting Less than Ten Years

If a couple is married for ten years or longer, a spouse is entitled to receive half of the higher-earning spouse's Social Security once the higher-earning spouse retires. Social Security payments for the higher-earning spouse are unaffected. It is troubling that the average length of marriage for people who get divorced is 9.6 years. Waiting just six months longer will increase the lower-earning spouse's retirement options.

Collection Rules in Detail

To collect on an ex-spouse's account, you must be unmarried and at least sixty-two. As long as you have been divorced for more than two years you can collect on an ex-spouse's account—even if your ex is still working—provided he or she has reached age sixty-two and is fully eligible for benefits. You do not have to wait two years if your ex-spouse is entitled to and receiving Social Security.

You can file an application for divorced spouse's benefits and receive up to one-half of their benefit amount unless you can get a bigger payment based on your own work history. As an example, let's assume your ex is receiving monthly Social Security benefits of $2,000 and based on your own work record you are entitled to a monthly benefit of $800. When you file for divorced spouse's benefits, you will be able to collect an additional $200 from the benefit record of your ex for a total of one-half of the ex's benefit. If you don't have your own benefits, you would receive $1,000 from your ex's earnings record.

How Remarriage Affects Benefits

The remarriage of an ex-spouse will not affect whether you are entitled to receive half of the benefit. And the amount an ex-spouse will receive has no effect on the benefit amount for his or her new spouse. In fact, if your ex gets divorced a second time, and the marriage has lasted more than ten years, that ex-spouse is also eligible for benefits.

Your remarriage (to someone other than your ex) will end your divorced spouse's benefits. If you remarry and that marriage ends (death, divorce, or annulment), you may be able to have benefits paid again based on your former spouse's record.

What If Your Ex Dies?

If your ex dies, the rules change slightly. Widow(er)s and surviving divorced spouse benefits may begin at age sixty. Also, if you are a divorced widow(er), you may continue to collect benefits if you remarry at age sixty or later, or at age fifty after you have become disabled.

Privacy rules prohibit Social Security from giving you an ex's earnings record, but the Social Security office can tell you what benefits you may be entitled to after you establish that you are the ex-spouse. Visit your local office or call 1-800-772-1213 for more information.

Understanding How It Affects You

As part of our divorce planning practice we take a close look at Social Security to make sure it is accounted for properly. A special retirement analysis is run that factors in the length of the marriage ensuring your Social Security projections are accurate. I recommend you work with a CDFA™ or another financial planner skilled in divorce issues to give you the guidance you need.

For more information go to the Social Security website at
http://www.socialsecurity.gov/retire2/divspouse.htm

Actions to Take Now

- $ Find your Social Security statement and become familiar with its provisions for your retirement.

- $ If you are not quite married ten years, speak with your attorney about the value in delaying your divorce until you qualify for spousal benefits.

- $ If you are working with a financial coach have them illustrate how Social Security factors into your long-term financial life. You can vary assumptions on you and your spouse's work life and retirement age and see how Social Security payments will contribute to your retirement.

CHAPTER 17

Retirement Assets

"Musicians don't retire;
They stop when there's no more music in them."
—*Louis Armstrong*

Retirement assets such as Individual Retirement Accounts (IRAs), 401(k)s, and pensions often make up the lion's share of a family's net worth. Unfortunately, they are also among the most improperly managed assets during divorce.

The feature that makes them excellent vehicles for retirement, favorable tax treatment, is also the feature that can cause fits during a divorce proceeding. You MUST take caution when dividing these assets.

I will describe for you the basic categories of retirement plans and then discuss some of the mistakes often made when dealing with them.

Types of Retirement Assets

There are many forms of retirement assets. And you may own some that are not mentioned here by name. But there are three major categories:

- 💰 Employer-based "qualified" plans
  - ✦ 401(k), 403(b), profit sharing plans
  - ✦ Pension plans
  - ✦ Employee stock purchase plans

- 💰 Individual retirement accounts such as traditional and Roth IRAs

- 💰 Insurance products such as variable and fixed annuities

There are many more retirement plan types not found as frequently, such as money purchase plans, cash balance pension plans, thrift plans, and IRAs (SIMPLE, SARSEP, and SEP IRAs).

If you have funds in these plans, you will want to consult a tax professional or your divorce financial analyst to learn about how these assets might be best handled in your divorce.

Qualified Plans

The term "qualified" relates to the Employee Retirement Income Security Act (ERISA) of 1974, which created the entire category of employer-based retirement plans we are all familiar with today. A retirement plan is qualified if it complies with the rules set forth in the ERISA. It allows employers to claim their retirement plan contributions as expenses and also allows the employee to defer paying taxes on their contributions until they retire. This double tax deduction is what makes these plans so attractive for employers and employees.

401(k), 403(b), and Profit Sharing Plans

These are by far the most common employer-based retirement assets to be divided during divorce. The typical 401(k) account is a combination of employee pre-tax contributions (from their paycheck) and employer matching contributions. The employer may also make additional profit sharing contributions, although this is less common today. 403(b)s are similar to 401(k)s but are used by tax-exempt organizations such as schools, hospitals, and religious groups.

Pensions

This rapidly vanishing retirement plan guarantees an income for the life of the employee, and potentially their spouse, based on years of service and overall employer and employee contributions. It is called a "defined benefit" plan, much like Social Security, in that the employee's benefit is defined not as a lump sum cash value but as an annual payment for life. Pensions need to be handled very carefully, as you will see.

Employee Stock Purchase Plans

These plans allow the employees to purchase company stock at a discount. They come in a qualified version, which gives tax deferral benefits like all qualified plans, and a nonqualified version.

Individual Retirement Accounts (IRAs)

IRAs are accounts that are managed by the account owner, not the employer. They come in two basic varieties: traditional tax-deferred IRAs and tax-free Roth IRAs.

Traditional tax-deferred IRAs contain assets that were made up of annual contributions by the account owner. They may also contain assets that were transferred from an employer plan such as a 401(k), in which case they are called "rollover" IRAs. The funds are *tax-deferred*, meaning they grow without tax impact until withdrawn, hopefully during retirement.

Tax-free Roth IRAs are special in that they are funded with money that has already been taxed, as opposed to pre-tax dollars that fund traditional IRAs. They are *tax-free* investments at withdrawal, assuming you follow certain rules.

Insurance and Annuity Products

Annuities are odd ducks in the investment world. They are complicated, confusing, and will make your eyes glaze over if you dig into the contracts too deeply. They come in the form of "variable" and "fixed" annuities[25] and are offered by life insurance companies.

---

25   There are many forms of annuities but these are the most common. Some 403(b) retirement plans, such as those offered by TIAA-CREF, have an annuity component to their retirement savings program. Annuity investments require careful analysis to determine how they are best managed in a divorce settlement.

Fixed annuities pay a fixed amount at retirement based on a stated interest rate, and so have characteristics similar to a bank CD (without the FDIC protection). Variable annuities have an investment component allowing you to invest in a portfolio of securities called subaccounts. Assets grow tax deferred until withdrawal at retirement.

Annuity taxation is similar to the taxation of IRAs with penalties for early withdrawal.

Common Divorce Mistakes with Retirement Plans

There are so many mistakes people make in handling retirement assets it is hard to know where to start. But there are three basic categories of mistakes we see all the time:

- Not accounting for taxes and penalties that may be due upon withdrawal

- Not calculating the value of a pension plan accurately

- Taking retirement assets as the bulk of your settlement.

Not Accounting for Taxes and Penalties

You have heard the joke, "What is heavier…a pound of feathers or a pound of lead?" Well, of course they both weigh the same…a pound. Unfortunately, it is not the same way with retirement and other assets.

It is not what you get in the divorce that matters; it is what you keep! If it were a house, it would be after selling and fix-up costs (plus annual maintenance). In the case of retirement assets, it is *after taxes and penalties are paid.*

Taxes

While employer retirement plans and IRAs are wonderful vehicles for accumulating tax-deferred wealth, they may lose a lot of value to taxes when withdrawn. Any distributions you make are added to your other taxable income and the total is subject to income tax. When you factor in both federal and state tax it is possible to pay as much as 45 percent in tax for every dollar withdrawn.

Penalties

In general, if funds are withdrawn before the age of 59½, there is another 10 percent additional tax that will be assessed. This can make the actual value of a 401(k) plan worth only half of its original value depending on the circumstances and tax bracket of the person withdrawing the funds.

Two Important Exceptions

Certain employer-based retirement accounts such as 401(k)s are not subject to tax when being divided as part of a divorce property settlement. The non-employee spouse can receive funds into his or her own retirement account (IRA) without taxes taken out if the assets are being divided through a Qualified Domestic Relations Order (QDRO).

In addition the spouse can receive some of these assets as a *withdrawal*, that is, put the funds in his or her savings account for spending purposes and *not pay the 10-percent penalty*.

Not Calculating Pensions Accurately

Pensions are some of the most overlooked and misunderstood assets. Some couples ignore them entirely not realizing their immense value.

Quick Quiz…

What is worth more, $250,000 in cash that you get today that you can invest at 4 percent per year, or a pension that pays you $15,000 per year for twenty years that grows 2.5 percent per year?

Believe it or not the value of the pension if you could take it all today would be $316,737…$66,000 more than the lump sum![26]

Pensions need to be evaluated carefully in a divorce proceeding. A financial analyst will be able to calculate for you the hypothetical value of a pension as if it were something you could get your hands on today.

Some of the factors that go into determining a value are:

- How much of the pension was earned during the marriage?

- How many years before the spouse who owns the pension retires?

- What is the estimated payment per year and any cost of living increase?

- How long will the payments last based on projected life expectancy?

---

26   In this simplified example we ignore taxes and practical considerations such as needing the funds today vs. over a twenty-year period. There are many considerations in deciding whether taking a pension is a wise choice.

Your CDFA™ will come up with a projected total value of payments to be paid out, and then do a separate calculation called a "present value" to arrive at a figure that gives you the equivalent value in today's dollars.

Finally, there is a calculation made to determine how much of the pension is a marital asset using something called the *coverture fraction*. The numerator represents the total period of time the pension holder participated in the plan during the marriage, and the denominator is the total period of time they participated in the plan as of the cutoff date (the valuation date). It is then that you can make a decision as to how you wish to handle the pension in your settlement agreement.

Taking Retirement Assets as the Bulk of Your Settlement

It is important to have *balance* where possible in the portfolio of assets received in your divorce. Whether you have it all in your home or your retirement accounts, too much of one type of asset is not a good thing.

Retirement assets are not meant for spending *today*. They are "tomorrow" assets. The government has set up the tax code to make it very expensive for you to tap these assets early.

So strive for balance: cash for spending today, investments for pre-retirement needs, and tax-advantaged retirement assets for retirement.

Strategies for Handling Pensions in Divorce

Knowing the value of the pension allows you to determine the best way to take the value in your settlement. There are two ways to handle pensions:

🝢 Participate in the income when the pension is paid out at retirement

$ Take an offsetting amount of other assets in place of the value of your share of the current pension.[27]

Participate in the Income at Retirement

Some pension plans will allow you to participate in the pension income benefit at your ex-spouse's retirement age. The advantage of this approach is that you will have an additional income stream at retirement you cannot outlive. However, the disadvantages are numerous:

$ Your spouse may die before collecting benefits, and you may get nothing.

$ Your spouse may remarry, which some companies will look at as superseding your rights.

$ Your spouse may leave the firm or retire before the divorce paperwork gets to the company, in which case the company has no (current) employee pension to modify.

$ You could need the funds before your ex retires.

It is extremely important to learn whether the pension administrator will allow for payments to be made to an ex-spouse, and to get the QDRO paperwork to them BEFORE *the divorce is finalized!*

This means getting the QDRO paperwork to the company, not just a judge, well before your divorce is complete. There have been instances

---

27   Many divorces, too many, arrange for the pension owner to keep his or her pension, while the other party keeps the house. This could be a big mistake, especially if the home is expensive to maintain.

where a QDRO was put in place after the divorce was final and the ex-spouse retired before the company received the QDRO. The result… no pension benefits for the non-employee spouse no matter what the agreement said.

Your lawyer will help you craft the language that will give you the protection you desire, but here are some of the more common provisions found in agreements relating to pension payouts:

- The receiving spouse should be named as beneficiary of the pension until the QDRO is complete.

- It specifies what will happen if the spouse dies before the QDRO is complete.

- It specifies what happens to the pension plan benefits if the employee dies before AND after retirement (these are two separate issues).

Take an Offsetting Amount of Assets

I am a fan of this option. It is not for everyone, because there are some situations where taking a lifetime income simply makes the most sense. But in general there are a lot of advantages to this approach:

- The value is received today, not years from now.

- There is no need to monitor your ex-spouse's plans for retirement.

- There is no tricky QDRO paperwork to prepare or complex clauses to put in your agreement to account for every eventuality associated with the future pension.

I don't want to minimize the value of a pension; an income for life is wonderful. If you feel you absolutely want to have this type of guarantee, there are annuity insurance products that will give you similar benefits.

It is essential before you buy an annuity product that you understand it completely. Annuities can be expensive to own and complicated in their design. Some also carry the risk of loss of principal. Still, they are the only investment that can give you an income stream for your lifetime, no matter how long you live.[28]

Actions to Take Now

- Gather all statements for retirement assets.

- Call your spouse's employer to learn of any and all retirement programs, including pensions.
  - Ask them for a recent statement.
  - If they won't provide one, ask your spouse or your attorney to work on getting one for you.

- Consider whether it would be more appropriate for you to have the guaranteed income stream at retirement or the equivalent in assets as part of your divorce settlement.

- If you work with a divorce financial analyst they can help you make smart decisions when it comes to dividing retirement assets. They can

---

28 Of course you can invest in bonds, bank CD's and other interest bearing securities, but the income will be less. Annuities pay a portion of your principal back to you in each payment so your total cash flow is greater.

+ Run a formal pension valuation for you

+ Project your retirement income based on various ways of dividing assets, Social Security, pension, and all other sources of income

+ Give you a year-by-year projection of your cash flow and net worth from the day of your divorce until the end of your life

+ Analyze your annuity contracts so you know how they work and summarize the pros and cons of having them in your settlement.

CHAPTER 18

Executive Compensation and Non-Qualified, Employer-Based Plans

"Half of all marriages end in divorce—
And then there are the really unhappy ones."
—Joan Rivers

When I was growing up I had a friend whose father worked for one of the big Fortune 500 companies. He was a big deal: white haired, ridiculously tall, baritone voice, and drove an Oldsmobile that always looked like it came off the showroom floor. He was what we all used to picture when we heard the word "executive."

That was in the 1960s, and so much has changed. The executive ranks of companies are now more diverse: younger, multicultural, and filled with people wearing polo shirts and khakis. Along with this trend is a change in the way valued employees get paid, with more people participating in compensation programs formerly reserved for only the most senior management.

These compensation programs are in the "other" category—neither salary nor traditional savings plans. They are "non-qualified" and therefore don't need to conform to the stringent rules set forth in the Employer Retirement Income Security Act of 1974, which cover 401(k)s and profitsharing plans.

They range from simple stock purchase plans to complex stock-option, restricted-stock, and deferred-compensation programs and deserve special attention. They are not easily understood and these days can be a significant part of the net worth of a growing number of households.

What Makes These Programs Unique?

This category of marital asset is unusual in the following ways:

- They may not be divisible between spouses, unlike most 401(k) and retirement accounts.

- Some states may not recognize them as a marital asset depending on the particular plan and circumstances.

- Many of these plans are tied to the employee's continued employment with the firm.

- Some plans have values tied to the future performance of a company's stock price, which can vary greatly over time, making the value difficult, if not impossible, to predict.

- Employees may not be entitled to the proceeds for years after they are first awarded.

So, in addition to the usual questions dealt with in a divorce settlement, you have these layers of uncertainty. But these types of accounts need to be evaluated carefully as their value can be substantial.

Types of Non-Qualified Employer Plans

There are several common types of non-qualified employer plans you might run into.

- 💰 Employee stock purchase plans

- 💰 Stock option plans

- 💰 Restricted stock plans

- 💰 Deferred compensation plans

Employee Stock Purchase Plans

These plans grant an employee the right to buy stock in the employer corporation at a discount, typically 15 percent off the market price. There is also a version that falls under the qualified plan rules discussed in the previous chapter.

Stock Option Plans

A stock option is a right granted to an employee to purchase shares in the company's stock at a predetermined price sometime in the future. They can represent a sizeable amount of wealth if the company's stock rises from the date they are granted. Unfortunately, they can also be worthless if the shares have not risen in value.

For instance, an employee may receive a grant of 1,000 options of ABC Company giving the employee the option to buy the shares (also known as exercising the option) beginning five years from now at today's price of $50 per share. If five years from now the stock is trading for $75 per share, the employee could purchase the shares at $50 from the company, then immediately sell them for $75, netting a gross profit of $25,000! If the shares are trading at $45, then the value of the options are $0. Aye, there's the rub with stock options. Feast or famine!

Stock options come in two varieties: incentive stock options and non-qualified stock options. The major difference is in the tax treatment with incentive stock options having potentially lower taxes when exercised and liquidated.

> *This is one area where you must consult with an accountant or other tax professional so you understand exactly what the after-tax value of these options may be worth under various scenarios. Your CDFA™ can also run a stock option analysis for you.*

Restricted Stock Plans

These are plans typically reserved for senior management. They are issued as either shares of stock or restricted stock units (RSUs), in which case the shares will be delivered at a future date. Under a restricted stock program, an employee is awarded stock that is subject to certain restrictions of transferability and to a substantial risk of forfeiture for a specific period of time.

"Substantial risk of forfeiture" is a legal term that means the risk that the employee will not receive the shares unless certain events occur. These may be time based, such as needing to be employed until a certain date in the future, or performance based, such as the revenue or profit growth of the firm. Of course, this raises the question about whether something that may or may not have a value can even be included in a divorce settlement. More on this in a moment!

Deferred Compensation Plans

This is additional compensation to be received by the employee at a date in the future. It is an unsecured promise to pay by the corporation, meaning the company needs to stay in business in order for it to be received. It is typically restricted to key employees.

Deferred compensation programs come under a variety of labels. They can be deferred bonus plans, supplemental executive retirement plans, or excess benefit plans. All of them have the same general construction.

Unique Issues with Executive Compensation

Issue #1: Determining If It Is a Marital Asset

One of the tricky parts in handling these compensation plans in a divorce settlement is the potential for disagreement as to whether they are a marital asset subject to division.

The following questions should help you gauge whether assets such as restricted stock are a marital asset:

- Was the compensation earned during the marriage? If it was earned prior to the marriage, it may be completely or at least partially excluded.

- Was the asset given based on past or future performance? Generally a court excludes compensation for services that will be performed after the marriage is dissolved.

- How far in the future before the stock options or restricted stock become available to the employee for sale (also known as "vested"). Some states will not consider stock or stock options that did not vest by the separation date or final divorce decree.

- How substantial is "the substantial risk of forfeiture"? The higher the likelihood the value will not be received, the more a judge may decide to not include it as a marital asset.

- How do the courts in your state treat these types of plans? There is wide variation state to state, and even judge to judge.

Keep in mind that a court has the ability, within their state guidelines, to award any amount of the marital property as it deems necessary and proper. That said, the restricted stock could be given to the employee, the employee spouse, or divided between the two.

Issue #2: Determining Value

Once it is determined that the compensation plan is subject to division as a marital asset, a value has to be assigned. This is simple in the case of publicly traded company stock but quite complex in the case of closely held private company stock and stock options.

Non-Publicly Traded Stock

If the stock purchase or stock option program is for a firm that has no publicly traded stock, a business valuation must be made by a trained expert. There are a number of methods (described in chapter 20) to come up with a fair estimate of the business's value as a whole. Once this is determined an estimated value for the employee's shares can be calculated.

Stock Options

Unlike a publicly traded stock purchase plan where you can assign a value by looking up the stock price as of a certain date, a stock option only has value if it allows you to buy shares of stock at a price lower than the market value at that time.

Stock options can be difficult to value in a divorce settlement. For many long-term employees there could be dozens of stock option awards accumulated over the years. For those options that can't be exercised today some may be "in the money," where a profit would hypothetically be made, while others may be worthless due to their exercise price being above the current market price. The question is how do you value an option that is worth nothing today but could have significant value in the future?

Every state has adopted an approach to value stock options. Some simply look at the *hypothetical profit* that would be made if the options could all be exercised at the same time as of a particular date (such as date of separation). They then figure out the marital portion of those options and award a percentage to the non-employee spouse. Simple? Yes. Fair? Maybe.

One advantage in using this approach is that it has *finality* and the receiving spouse acquires assets they may not otherwise receive. One disadvantage is that this valuation is *totally hypothetical.* In actuality, the options will be worth more or less at the time they are exercised. So the risk and reward is all on the employee spouse once the divorce is finalized. He or she may have paid out assets that are based on worthless stock options or reap a windfall.

Another approach is to have a trained specialist conduct a sophisticated and complex valuation using something called the *Black/Scholes* model. This only works with publicly traded securities and attempts to factor in variables including the time and price volatility.

Neither of these approaches is ideal. As a result, many courts opt to have the risks and rewards shared between the spouses. This is accomplished by having an "if and when received agreement" as described below.

Issue #3: Figuring Out How to Divide These Plans

Courts have two approaches in dealing with these assets in a divorce. The first reassigns ownership to the non-employee spouse, while the second has the non-employee spouse receive the asset value at a later date.

Direct Division

Some, though not many, non-qualified plans can be divided in divorce, so that the non-employee spouse gets his or her share directly from the plan. If the non-qualified plan does not allow for division in a divorce, he or she may be looking at an "if and when received" agreement.

'If and When Received' Agreement

This is popular in divorce settlements for stock and stock option programs where a future value is simply not possible to calculate.

This is an agreement that identifies how the amounts will be divided after the divorce—*if and when* the employee takes distributions from the plan. Language would be put in the settlement that describes the timing for exercising stock options and sale of restricted stock units, how taxes will be paid, and how proceeds will be distributed to the ex-spouse.

This settlement language must be carefully crafted.
You should consult with your attorney and advisor team
to make sure the language reflects your interests, and to
understand the pros and cons of using this form of compensation
arrangement rather than an upfront payout.

Actions to Take Now

- Collect information on any and all executive compensation programs owned by you or your spouse, including those earned from a previous employer.

- Review these programs thoroughly and work with a financial coach and attorney to determine how they might be incorporated into your settlement agreement.

- If you are working with a financial coach they can:

  - Read through company documents and summarize them, explain how they work, and identify what issues there may be with them in a divorce settlement

+ Run hypothetical illustrations for you and your attorney or mediator showing you what the value may be based on any variety of assumptions, including market price, timing, and taxation

+ Show you how taking the funds now as an upfront payout may benefit you versus an "if and when received" approach.

If there ever were a place for caution, it is in evaluating these nontraditional plans. Take your time and get the advice of your team before making decisions.

CHAPTER 19

Guaranteeing Your Settlement With Life Insurance

"There are worse things in life than death.
Have you ever spent an evening with an insurance salesman?"
—*Woody Allen*

There are a lot of really great people in the insurance business, so please excuse the Woody Allen quote, which pokes fun at the stereotype of the nagging insurance salesman. Life insurance is an essential part of wealth management and our financial lives would be much more at risk without it.

Life insurance is usually one of the last items to be agreed upon during negotiation and often isn't discussed at all. This leaves critical financial commitments such as child support, spousal support (alimony), and other obligations totally at risk should the income provider die.

Existing life insurance policies purchased during the marriage may stay in place if there is an assurance that they will remain in force with the ex-spouse as a beneficiary. But here are some ways that you can increase your chances of having insurance there when you need it.

Make Sure Your Settlement Contains Specific Insurance Language
In your divorce negotiations your attorney should advocate for specific language in your agreement that clearly defines the type and length of insurance coverage. It should specify which existing insurance should stay in place and whether the owner or beneficiaries should be changed. It should also say what new insurance needs to be acquired to guarantee spousal or child support obligations.

The Beneficiary Should Become the Owner, If Possible
The owner of the policy controls the right to determine who the beneficiaries are and makes the payments on the policy. It is prudent in a divorce agreement to direct that the beneficiary become the owner of insurance policies. That way beneficiaries relying on the insurance coverage can be sure that premiums will continue to be paid and the policy will remain in effect.

As the owner you will receive premium and lapse notices, and only you can cancel the policy.

You May Buy a Policy on Your Ex-spouse's Life
If your insurance company will not allow an ownership change, you can apply for insurance on your ex-spouse's life and name yourself as beneficiary. You can also name your children as next-in-line (contingent) beneficiaries if you were to pass away before your spouse.

You will need to demonstrate to the insurance company that you have a legitimate need for the insurance (an insurable interest), and your ex will need to participate in acquiring the insurance through answering medical questions and other information required on the application.

What Type of Insurance to Buy

Insurance comes in two basic varieties that are applicable to divorce agreements.

The first is *term insurance* which, as the name suggests, only gives coverage for a limited time. The second is *whole life insurance* which, as you might expect, is paid for the entire life of the owner and has a cash value accumulation feature built in.

Most agreements use term life insurance as the preferred option because it is low cost and the coverage can be timed to coincide with the payment obligation of the ex-spouse. As an example, if child support ends in ten years, you can purchase a ten-year policy with fixed premiums.

An insurance specialist or CDFA™ should be consulted to review your existing policies and determine the amount and type of coverage that is best for you, and if new policies need to be acquired.

Trusts as Beneficiaries

If your spouse has significant financial obligations and wants to control how the assets are paid out after death, it may make sense to have a trust as beneficiary.

A trust document can specify how the assets may be spent, the timing of payments, and special provisions to make certain the funds are used in the way they were intended by the donor. As an example, the death benefit can be designated to be used for college expenses only or can be paid as the child reaches specified ages.

Disability and Other Insurance

Other insurance that may be relevant is disability insurance. It is much more likely that a breadwinner will become unable to work for a period of time than they are to die. Therefore, it may make sense to have disability insurance to help cover their obligations.

Actions to Take Now

- Gather all life insurance contracts and review them carefully. The contracts should include insurance offered by employers.

- Have a conversation with your mediator or attorney about the need to have income payments protected should your spouse die or become disabled.

- Become the owner of existing policies, if possible.

- If new policies are required, meet with a qualified insurance professional to get quotes.

CHAPTER 20

Dealing with Business Interests

"I love being married. It's so great to find that one special person you want to annoy for the rest of your life."
—*Rita Rudner*

When I was a kid I never realized how many families in my neighborhood were business owners. There was Bill's mom who ran a hair salon, my dad's friend who ran a small manufacturing firm two towns over, and the annoying kid down the street whose father had an insurance agency. The annoying kid of course ended up being the most successful of all of us. Dang.

Many families have an earner who is self-employed or works for a firm in which he or she is a significant owner. Whether it is a medical practice, a single-person consultancy, or a family-owned manufacturer, these business interests are among the most contentious and difficult-to-deal-with assets in a divorce settlement.

Dividing a business as part of a divorce isn't easy—almost impossible, actually—without selling it outright. And, as you will see, there are many special considerations that make this an area of your agreement deserving attention and care.

I strongly suggest you work with your advisor team to get an early understanding about how you might handle division of a business interest. In addition to the usual questions of whether it is a marital asset, it raises unique issues that complicate its treatment in a divorce.

How Are Business Interests Different?

Business interests require more attention than other assets because:

- They aren't easily sold

- Their values require special analysis and are somewhat subjective

- They are often owned with other people.

A Business Can Be Difficult to Sell

Unlike your retirement and investment accounts, and even your home, a business is tough to sell, especially quickly. Depending on the business there may be a limited market, especially if you and your spouse own a non-controlling interest of less than 50 percent.

Determining a Value Requires Special Analysis

Business valuation is a subspecialty of the accounting field and requires special training. Valuing a business is not a simple matter of looking it up online or doing a standard appraisal as you might do for your family home.

It requires making a number of assessments and, at best, is an estimate of how much a qualified buyer would be willing to pay for the business.

Many subjective judgments must be made by the business valuation expert in arriving at a valuation conclusion. It is rare that two business valuation experts arrive at the exact same conclusion about value.

They Are Often Owned with Other People

If the business is owned with other partners, things can get especially messy. For instance, there may be a prohibition against the transfer of shares without the approval of the other partners. As a protective measure partners may also have required that a prenuptial agreement be put in place in which new spouses waive their right to direct ownership in the business. If you signed a prenuptial agreement, you should see if there is language that you may be bound to.

Ways of Valuing a Business

There are three approaches to valuing a business interest: the asset approach, the income approach, and the market approach.

The *asset approach* presents a value of all tangible assets such as buildings, inventory, cash, and machinery, and intangible assets such as trademarks, goodwill, and copyrights.

An *income-based approach* determines a value using one or more methods that convert anticipated income streams into a single dollar amount. It is the most widely recognized approach to valuing an interest in a privately held business. There are several methodologies within the income approach.

A *market-based approach* compares the business to similar businesses that have been sold, much like a home appraisal. Valuing a business in this way is often problematic as it can be challenging to find businesses similar enough to one another to make a valuation credible.

Goodwill

Many times the value of a business is significantly higher than the value of its assets. This is called "goodwill" and comes in two forms: personal and enterprise.

"Personal" goodwill is the portion directly associated with the person running or working in the business. As an example, if a lawyer in a law firm is a well-known and sought-after attorney, he may have significant personal goodwill.

Goodwill of the "enterprise" is attached to the business itself, not the person. If the valuation has substantial enterprise goodwill, it is likely to be considered a marital asset as it will exist even if the person is no longer with the firm.

You need to consult your state's laws on how goodwill is treated. Often judges will consider personal goodwill not subject to division but will consider enterprise goodwill divisible as a marital asset.

Ways of Handling Business Interests

Once you have established that a business interest is subject to division in a divorce and have arrived at a market value, you need to decide how to treat it in your settlement. There are three basic approaches:

- 💰 You can stay involved in the business as a partner. Some couples can do this, some cannot. And as I just mentioned there may be other owners who have a say in this.

- 💰 You can use other marital assets such as stocks, cash, real estate, and retirement funds to pay the non-employee spouse his or her share of the value of the business.

- 💰 You can structure a property settlement note—this is a multiyear payout with interest.

- 💰 You can sell the business and divide the net selling price.

Which solution is right for you depends on many factors. These include the availability of assets to fund a buyout, contractual constraints in the form of prenuptial and partner agreements, and whether you wish to be involved in the business. You must speak with your attorney about your options based on the particulars of your situation.

Has the Business Been 'Divorce Proofed'?

There are books showing business owners how to "divorce proof" their business so their value is protected should the owner become divorced.[29]

These are often legitimate and legal strategies but, if you feel you are being treated unfairly, you will want your attorney to take a closer look on your behalf as to what may have been done to take assets off the table that might be rightfully yours.

---

29   Fellow author Jeff Landers' has written extensively on this topic in his book "How to Divorce-Proof Your Business".

Some of these strategies are:

- 💰 Drawing a ridiculously high salary so that the assets of the business look smaller than they are

- 💰 Putting agreements in place prohibiting spousal ownership (we just talked about this)

- 💰 Moving you out of direct involvement in the business so you appear less of a contributor to its success, even if it is to manage the home and children so your spouse can be more effective at work

- 💰 Moving jointly held assets of the business into his or her name alone

- 💰 Hiding company assets in accounts not easily discovered.

If you are suspicious that any of these might be happening, your attorney can hire a forensic accountant to look over the business's books to ensure everything is as it should be.

Making a Business Look Less Valuable

While we all would love to trust our spouse, divorce has a way of bringing out the worst in people. One way a spouse may try to get an unfair financial advantage is by making a business they own look less valuable than it actually is.

A forensic accountant is often employed to review the financial records of a business to validate that nothing has been done to reduce its perceived value. Some things they look for include:

- 💰 Employing friends or family for fake jobs to set aside funds for themselves

- Reducing cash balances and profits by making unusual investments in inventory, cars, or buildings

- Not collecting on customer payments that are due (cash receivables)

- Anything that will make the firm appear less profitable.

A forensic accountant will also look at past tax returns and perhaps even interview some of the employees to get a sense of whether anything out of the ordinary is happening.

Actions to Take Now

If you or your spouse are owner or part owner of a privately held firm, you should have a conversation with your attorney about how to treat the value of the business in your settlement. You should ask about whether it is likely to be a marital asset, how best to determine its value, and the most effective way to deal with it in negotiations.

If you are working with a financial coach they can simplify the decision of how to treat a business interest in your agreement. They have specialized software which can:

- Model any payment plan, buyout, or sale and show you how it may affect your cash flow and net worth for years to come

- Show you the practical impact of taking other assets in place of business ownership

- Test out various strategies to see which ones are most advantageous including:

+ Sharing ownership of the business and taking annual income
+ Phasing out of the business over time
+ Taking an installment payment in place of your ownership interest.

Chapter 21

Refining and Finalizing Your Agreement

"All marriages are happy. It's the living together afterward that causes all the trouble."
—*Raymond Hull*

Building a financial settlement is a lot like building a house. You start with the foundation and end with deciding what color to paint the guest bathroom, going step by step, basics to details, until you have created something that is right for you when you look at it in its entirety.

Along the way you monitor your progress and make adjustments. You consider proposals for items like fixtures, flooring, and windows and determine what fits your needs and overall vision. You must do the same with financial proposals as you build your settlement.

Eight Questions to Help You Assess Proposals

If you are using a financial analyst/coach, you will have illustrations and projections to help you see the long-term benefits of any proposal. But even if you have reams of data and charts you need to interpret what they mean. So below are eight questions to ask yourself as you compare any two alternatives:

- Which one is worth more to me once all taxes and other costs are factored in?
  + Taxes and penalties can take a big bit out of 401(k)s and tax-deferred investments while other assets like real estate are relatively tax privileged.

- When do I receive the assets?
  + Sooner is better than later, other things being equal. You want control of the asset as soon as possible.

- Is one more certain to be received than the other?
  + Some assets like stock options, may or may not have value in the future if the stock price tanks or your ex-spouse leaves the company.

- Which alternative gets me the assets when I need them most?
  + If you receive assets over time, are they timed to coincide with major expenses such as college?

- Which one is more liquid and can be turned into spendable cash earlier and at least cost?
  + A home may be a great investment but takes time to sell. Same thing with partial ownership of a private company or other business interest.

ⓢ Which one has better growth potential? What are the odds it will grow the way I expect it to?

✦ If it is a long-term asset like real estate, what is the market outlook? What is the worst-case scenario?

ⓢ Which one adds the most balance to my agreement?

✦ You want to have an agreement that has a mix of cash assets, long-term investments, and tax-deferred investments for retirement. If you are overloaded in one area you may want to choose to diversify with other assets.

ⓢ Which one contributes best to my long-term cash flow and net worth?

✦ When you look at your agreement in its entirety over ten years, which alternative gives you better bottom-line cash flow and net worth?

I have included several tools to help you compare alternative proposals plus more detail and sample reports in the divorce planner guide. You can download it by clicking here or by going to www.divorcefinancialally.com/freefinancialplanner.

The Property vs. Alimony Decision

One of the more common decisions faced by divorcing couples is whether it is better to receive spousal support (alimony) over a number of years or additional property in its place. There are a number of considerations to think about as you make your decision:

ⓢ *Permanence*—Alimony is subject to change based on the circumstances of the spouses after the marriage is over. A change in incomes, retirement, employment, remarriage, cohabitation, and death can all result in raising, lowering, or terminating payments. Property settlements are commitments that stay in place even if one of the spouses dies.

💰 *Time value of money*—While it is good to have an income stream for an extended period of time, payments lose value to inflation over the years. With 3-percent inflation a dollar received today is only worth 74 cents ten years from now. A present-value calculation can be run by your CPA or CDFA™ to show you what would make payments over time equivalent to receiving a lump sum today.

💰 *Income needs*—Alimony is designed to help balance income between spouses and provide economic support over time. If there is a real need for regular income to pay bills and maintain a household, alimony may be a better choice than property, which might need to be liquidated.

Getting to the Final Agreement

Every divorce negotiation is different. Some are straightforward and simple and result in a completed settlement in short order. Others last months or years and result in agreements only after arduous negotiation or a decision by a judge. Personalities, financial complexity, and the method of divorce all factor into how long it takes to get to a final agreement both sides will accept.

If you have a good negotiation game plan, know your priorities, and are diligent about looking at all sides of each proposal, you will know when your agreement meets your standards. But while it is important to work towards a settlement that meets your needs, getting *everything* you want may be impossible. That is why you need to know your BATNAs and WATNAs.

BATNAs and WATNAs

How do you know how hard to push for getting something you really want in your settlement? One way is to look at the potential best and worst case outcomes should your case go to trial. Mediators call this your "Best Alternative to a Negotiated Agreement" (BATNA) and Worst Alternative to a Negotiated Agreement (WATNA) and is used as a tool to keep negotiations moving forward.

Based on his or her understanding of the facts of your case, the judge's past decisions, and your state's laws, your attorney should be able to tell you what the range of outcomes might be if your divorce settlement is decided in court. You can then gauge at what point you make a compromise, which while less than ideal, is far better than what a judge might decide.

Making the call to compromise requires that you be in touch with how negotiations are progressing and clarity as to what is really important to you. Only you, in consultation with your attorney and careful analysis of your agreement, can make the decision about when to make a concession.

In the following section we talk about how to review the draft of your finalized agreement.

Analyzing Your Completed Agreement

So after weeks or perhaps months of wrangling and negotiating, you have what seems to be a workable agreement. It gives you most of what you are looking for and on balance seems fair and equitable.

But one of the dangers of divorce is the overwhelming desire to just get it over with. Once you have painfully ground through all the big issues in the negotiations, it is common to begin glossing over the final details so that you can just call an end to the whole ordeal.

But this would be a mistake. Imagine putting up the frame of your dream house, going on vacation, and signing off on the project without seeing the finished home. You wouldn't, of course. That is why it is extremely important that you analyze and verify the agreement is right for you before you sign.

Does It Say What It Is Supposed to Say?

- Does the language clearly reflect what you want?

- Are all assets and debt accounted for?

- Does it say who is responsible for building the QDROs and documentation?

- Have you insured any promised income payments with life insurance?

I encourage you to reread chapter 11, "Five Tests Every Divorce Settlement Must Pass."

Is It the Right Agreement...for You?

A wonderfully crafted agreement may be a work of art but still not be right for you. Even if all the I's are dotted and the T's crossed, it will mean nothing if it does not give you what you need.

That is why I recommend you have a financial analyst give you a "final agreement summary package," which will show you in black and white the long term financial impact of your agreement. It will show you everything you need to know to be comfortable with the results of your hard work.[30]

The Final Agreement Summary Package

Your divorce financial advisor will prepare for you a series of summaries and analyses that will show you everything you need to know to be comfortable with your agreement. It will contain several reports:

What You Are Agreeing to...the Numbers

- Detailed lists of assets to be divided

- A division of marital property report

- Supporting documents that may include

    - Pension valuations

    - "What-if" illustrations

    - Alimony and child support

    - Home sale projections

    - Stock option vesting schedules

    - Budget information for each spouse

---

30   Your CDFA™ does not replace your attorney, and the final report package is not a legal document that binds any party. You should review all CDFA™ analyses with your attorney to ensure it accurately reflects what is stated in your property settlement agreement.

What It Potentially Means for Your Financial Future

- A ten-year cash flow and net worth projection for each spouse

- A net income and net worth spreadsheet showing year-by-year details

- Retirement projections

These reports will tell you what you have agreed upon, and give you a view of your financial life years down the road if you agree to the final settlement. Of course all projections are based on many assumptions, some of which may change, and therefore cannot be considered guarantees.

Questions to Ask Yourself as You Review the Package

- Is the after-tax division of assets close to 50/50?

- Will you have the income you need to support your lifestyle?

- Are you maintaining positive cash flow over time?

- Are there any assets unaccounted for?

- Is your net worth declining or growing each year?

- How does your net worth projection compare with your spouse's?

- Are the asset values accurate?

If you are not working with a divorce financial advisor, I encourage you to ask your lawyer or mediator for the reports I described above or find a local CPA or divorce planner who can take the contents of your agreement and give you the information you need.

Actions to Take Now

- Get a copy of the final divorce settlement and read it thoroughly.

- Make notes of any discrepancies from your understanding of what you agreed to.

- Meet with your financial coach, if you have one, to review the final agreement summary package he or she will have prepared for you.

- Meet with your attorney to discuss any concerns.

- If you have downloaded the free implementation guide go through the "pre-launch" questions to make sure you have not missed anything.

- Once you are satisfied, sign your settlement agreement.

STAGE 3

Recovery

CHAPTER 22

The Path to Recovery

"In three words I can sum up everything
I've learned about life: It goes on."
—*Robert Frost*

In my divorce I first moved into a small unfurnished home with ultra-white walls and a funky kitchen with an old rotary phone hanging by a tired fridge. Soon I had some furnishings and my things on the shelves, and it began to feel more like a home.

My three kids came over with our dog in hand every week, and gradually we built new rhythms into our lives. The adjustments kept coming, fast and furious at first, then more slowly. And they went on for some time until we no longer felt them anymore.

Recovery from divorce takes time. How much time depends on a lot of factors: the length of your marriage, the issues leading to the divorce, and your own personal psychology. But for most people it will take two to four years to get through it all.

The adjustments come as a shock at first, and then fade over time until you look back and say, "Wow...I feel normal again."

During this time you will have a lot to deal with. My job in this chapter is to help you manage through one important aspect of your recovery by giving you a step-by-step process for rebuilding all things related to money.

It is my hope that you will have more time for the other things in life, such as your family, your health, and all things connected with your peace of mind.

Why a Recovery Plan Is Important

For many people financial recovery happens slowly, painfully, and incompletely. Unfortunately, even leaving 10 percent of your financial to-do list undone can have huge consequences. What kind of consequences? Consider these:

- The forty-year-old woman who realized after her ex-husband's funeral that he removed her as beneficiary on a life insurance policy he was obligated to carry to pay for college expenses

- The fifty-five-year-old man who was cut out of his ex-wife's pension income because the paperwork was never filed properly and acted upon by her employer

🖐 The investment portfolio that lost 50 percent of its value in a stock market pullback because it was 100 percent invested in the same speculative growth stocks that were bought years ago and was never invested into more low-risk assets.

So a recovery plan is the final step, and perhaps the most important one. It is where you implement the life plan you have worked so hard to envision and develop. It makes what you imagine...real.

What Are the Elements of a Recovery Plan?

Your recovery plan has three parts: implementing your agreement, putting your financial house in order, and getting back to feeling good emotionally. My hope is that helping you with the first two will also help you move forward positively in your life and with the healing process overall.

Implementing your agreement sounds so simple. Just do it...right? It is all laid out in black and white, so just get it done. Well, unfortunately the divorce landscape is littered with poorly or partially implemented settlements. So we will help you make sure yours does not become one of them.

Getting your financial house in order is where the "new financial you" gets built. It encompasses all aspects of personal finance, including budgeting, investments, insurance, your estate plan, credit, and taxes.

Taking care of your emotional and physical self is perhaps most important of all. All the money in the world will not help you feel better if you have not taken the time and gotten the support you need to feel good again.

Time-Critical First Steps

Before you get into the nitty-gritty of your recovery plan there are a few items that simply can't wait. They need to be done *right away* to protect your and your family. To defer acting on them or to ignore them altogether is financial Russian roulette.

Change Accounts into Your Name

As you gather your papers, take note of the names in account titles. Anything in joint name with your ex needs to be changed to your name only unless you agreed otherwise. If you changed your name as a result of the divorce, you'll need to get a new Social Security card, driver's license, passport, and credit cards. You'll also need to notify your bank, utilities, insurance companies, credit card companies, the motor vehicle department, your children's school(s), etc., about any change of name or address. The titles on all assets, such as cars and houses, will have to be modified and recorded with mortgage companies.

Update Wills, Trusts, and Other Estate Documents

Make an appointment with your attorney and review your will or trust. In addition to redocumenting where your assets go after your death, you will want to think through who will be the guardians of your minor children and who will make health care decisions for you if you are unable to. Your attorney should walk through each document and point out areas you might want to change. I talk about this more in chapter 24.

Update Your Beneficiaries

After the divorce is final it is easy to forget to do something as important as redesignating who gets your money when you die. Your life insurance policies, IRA and 401(k) accounts, and wills and trusts may need to be changed. Call each firm to get the paperwork you need and fill it out carefully. It is generally best to avoid naming your "estate" as beneficiary; name real living people instead. Otherwise, the asset will become part of your willed estate and subject to the public court review process known as probate. This would likely delay the distribution of these assets to your heirs.

Get Life Insurance in Place

You need to have your family protected. If your ex is required to carry insurance as part of your agreement, you need to get confirmation the policy is in place. Ideally, you are now designated as the owner of the policy and will be getting copies of the statements so you can monitor whether the payments are current. Speak with an advisor to acquire new insurance if necessary on your own life.

Assemble Your Advisor Team

You need to make sure you have the help of a few key advisors. Your stable of professionals should include an attorney, financial planner/investment advisor, and a tax professional. Ask for referrals from people you trust. Your CDFA™ can also get you in touch with the firms that have reputations for competence, professionalism, and exceptional client service. Interview at least two in each category and work with the one you communicate with best and works with clients similar to you.

Actions to Take Now

- 🪙 Read through the time-critical first steps section above and make the updates suggested.

- 🪙 Assemble your advisor team.

- 🪙 If you are working with a CDFA™ in developing a recovery plan, he or she can refer you to people who can be a part of your advisor team. They will also help you identify the critical first steps most in need of attention.

CHAPTER 23

Creating Your Personal Financial Action Plan

"I love deadlines.
I like the whooshing sound they make as they fly by!"
—Douglas Adams

I love to-do lists. It is an art form of sorts to take out my favorite pen (a Uniball® Vision Elite) and spiral notebook and make lists of tasks neatly segmented into "work," "personal," and "other" categories. I even put little dots next to each task and an estimated time to complete. I know it's odd and a little obsessive compulsive but it works for me.[31] My kids find it weird.

But if you want to accomplish anything in life you must have a plan. Fuzzy plans yield fuzzy results. Good plans yield good results. In this

---

31   I have been known to even add unplanned activities I do during the day to my list just so I can cross them off.

chapter you will see how to build a plan for your financial life that will set you on the path toward the fresh start you desire.

Your personal recovery plan is a to-do list that ensures you will take the actions needed to reorganize your financial life the right way. It connects directly with your vision and the settlement agreement you built during negotiations; it is also the last step in this long saga called divorce.

If you follow these steps, what might take years to accomplish in an incremental hit-or-miss way will happen much more quickly, giving you the peace of mind that financial security brings.

There are three steps to building your recovery plan:

1. Get yourself organized

2. Dissect your agreement and identify actions to be taken or monitored

3. Create strategies for the six building blocks of personal financial security.

Get Yourself Organized

The Financial Freedom Binder

It is totally understandable that once the divorce is finalized you simply want to take a break from all the financial stuff, but it is important to reserve a little energy to get your new financial life in order.

I recommend you get a single binder for all important papers. When we work with our clients in their recovery plans we give them a binder with tabs for all the important papers. The binder has sections for estate planning, budgets, investments, and the other elements of a person's financial life. When it is time to talk about money matters everything is in one place.

Gather *all* of your account statements—from checking account to investment accounts to your company retirement plan, all of them. This is your "asset" information. Then do the same for your "liabilities," such as your mortgage, credit cards, car loans, and other debt. Create sections for all your divorce paperwork, insurance policies, and estate documents. Put it in a safe but accessible place since you will refer to it often.

Dissecting and Monitoring Your Agreement

Your agreement is a legal contract that can be simple or amazingly complicated. Either way, there are commitments both you and your spouse must take action on in order make your agreement a reality and to keep out of legal trouble.

You would think that given all the time and energy that goes into an agreement, putting it in place would be an easy, if not automatic, process. But that is simply not the case.

Lawyers can take their eye off the implementation ball as they move on to the next divorce case, and your mediator is not responsible for implementing agreements. So it is really important that you, whose financial life hinges on getting your agreement implemented properly, be on top of things.

Fortunately, there is a process for doing this. And it is simply to read your agreement, make a list of each action and commitment, and *create a tracking sheet* so you can keep tabs on what is to be done and by whom.

Agreements are a mass of words on white paper, and sometimes written in ways that are tough to decipher, but they generally contain four types of financial commitments:

- Asset division and transfer instructions

- Obligations to pay income or certain expenses

- Sale of assets and division of proceeds

- Obligations triggered by a future event

Let's go over each one.

Asset Division Instructions

The splitting up of marital assets are the bread and butter of settlement agreements. How this is accomplished varies depending on the type of asset being divided.

Investment, Checking, and Savings Accounts

If these are held in joint name, they are available to either owner. Therefore, it is a simple matter to open a separate account and transfer the agreed-upon amount to an account held in your name. If they are held in single name only, the account owner issues a directive to the bank or brokerage firm and the assets are transferred into the account.

Please note that *there are tax implications in liquidating investment assets* such as stocks, bonds, and mutual funds in taxable accounts. It may be beneficial to simply move the assets "in kind," which means to transfer a portion of the investments as-is (as IBM stock, for example), rather than sell them and move the cash proceeds.

You should consult with your tax and investment advisor as to what may be most appropriate for you from a tax perspective. In general, if the portfolio is a good one for you (see the section on investment portfolio considerations in chapter 25), a sale will just add unnecessary expense in the form of taxes and transactions costs.

Qualified Domestic Relations Order (or 'Quadro')

Some types of accounts, mainly retirement plans sponsored by corporations, can only be split through a formal order known as a QDRO. As was mentioned earlier this legal document is the formal authorization that instructs a company to transfer assets to a non-employee spouse as an "alternate payee" per a divorce settlement.

Assets that require a QDRO are "defined contribution" accounts like 401(k)s and "defined benefit" plans such as pensions. They are part of a group of corporate retirement plans regulated by the federal government under the Employee Retirement Income Security Act of 1974. We discussed these matters in chapter 16.

This is an area of divorce recovery that is littered with potential problems. These are legal documents often created by disconnected third parties requiring just the right wording so that appropriate action is taken by the employer.

As you might imagine there is the opportunity for delays and errors in the process, especially if what is being transferred involves complex assets such as pensions. So it is *essential* that you make note of what assets require a QDRO and monitor the process carefully (also see chapter 17 for more information about QDROs).

> *A QDRO is a complicated document dealing with the division of a complex investment. It is important that care be taken in structuring your agreement so that it is clear how these assets are to be divided and to monitor the creation of the QDRO so it conforms to your wishes.*

Other Types of Asset Splits

Individual retirement accounts (IRAs) do not require a QDRO. The brokerage or mutual fund firm holding the assets just need a "letter of instruction" from the account owner specifying that assets are to be moved to another party as part of a divorce agreement. They may have their own forms to simplify the transfer. If you don't have an IRA opened in your name, you will need to open one.

Executive compensation plans may or may not be divided subject to a divorce, depending on the rules of the corporation. These plans include deferred compensation, stock purchase plans, restricted stock grants, and stock option programs.

As part of building your agreement, and prior to your approval, you should have learned which of these plans, if any, could be split into accounts in your name. If they were not able to be placed in an account in your name, then you may have put in your agreement *"if and when received"* language that states what is to happen when the assets become available to the employee spouse.

Obligations to Provide Income or Pay Expenses

Alimony and child support payments, or commitments to pay expenses such as a mortgage or health care insurance, should be noted and tracked.

It is especially important where you are the beneficiary of a life insurance policy that you know when a payment has been made. Arrange to have duplicate statements sent to you or have the check deposited into an account you can monitor.

Sales of Assets and Division of Proceeds

If a home or other asset is going to be sold and the proceeds divided, you should make note of this. While it is unlikely you will forget about a home sale, there may be other assets that will call less attention to themselves, especially if the accounts are numerous and small. Small brokerage accounts, health savings accounts, and even frequent flyer miles you agree to split tend to vanish from consciousness unless special care is taken. Your CDFA™ can create a spreadsheet for you.

Obligations Based on a Future Event

There is nothing to do here except to understand clearly what will trigger a potential payment. Typical events include death, remarriage, termination of employment, retirement, or children reaching the age of majority.

Actions to Take Now

- Use the financial recovery "Personal Financial Action Plan" found in the back of this book and in the free "Financially Smart Divorce

Planner" you can download from our website by clicking here or going to www.divorcefinancialally.com/freefinancialplanner.

💰 In the front section you will see an area where you can make notes of action items relating to your agreement. It is broken down into sections for accounts to be opened, QDROs to be created, and so on. Simply make a note of each one that applies to you.

As you go through this next chapter, we will point out what should go in your action plan.

CHAPTER 24

Putting Together Your New Financial Life

"Faith is taking the first step even when
you don't see the whole staircase."
—*Martin Luther King Jr.*

In this chapter we will talk about what you need to do to reorganize your finances so you are in the best shape possible today and pave the way for future financial security.

There are four parts to a sound financial plan, and we will talk about each one in the next three chapters:

   🪙 Your spending plan and managing credit

   🪙 Estate planning and taxes

    💰 Investments

    💰 Insurance

We will cover investments and insurance in chapter 25. But for now let's go on to your spending plan and some of the actions you may want to take in the realm of estate planning and taxes.

Your Spending Plan

Budget...I can't think of a word that makes me cringe more. It has connotations of my Aunt Betty's frugality and is guaranteed to suck the fun out of any conversation, and life in general.

But we really need to look at budgeting differently. We should look at it as a way we make sure we get the important things we want out of life. And it does so by helping us spend our money wisely so we can have the joy and contentment we so desire for our entire lifetime.

So how do you build a budget? If you have been working with a divorce financial advisor throughout your divorce, it should be a simple matter of updating the estimates you put together during the preparation phase of this program.

If you are doing this for the first time on your own, use the worksheet in the appendix and you will see a budgeting tool that will help you get started on organizing your expenses.

Gather Your Data

Gather an entire year of statements from your bank and credit cards. Often you can download these into a spreadsheet directly, and sort them by where your money was spent. Try to use as much real data as possible...not what you think you may have spent. It is easy to miss the eight-dollar after work cocktail on workdays (over $2,000 per year!) or the weekly car wash.

As you go through your day, keep a journal of your expenses, especially those that are made in cash from the ATM.

Create a Spending Plan

Rather than thinking about "budgets," which seem so limiting, think about a "spending plan" that incorporates what you need to spend money on (nondiscretionary) and what you choose to spend money on (discretionary).

While there are probably limitations in the amount of money you have, you should still carve out spending on things that give you joy. It is cliché to say the "best things in life are free" like love, companionship, and the feeling of sun on your face, but most likely some of what you enjoy will cost money.

Finding out what is really important to you once you are single again is one of the greatest moments of enlightenment that will come from this life experience. I am not a therapist, or a yoga instructor, but in my experience there truly is an opportunity to become more grounded and happier by focusing on the few things that make us thrilled with life. By editing out the frivolous and unnecessary—whether this means things, activities, or even people—we become more content.

Establish Your Credit and Pay Down Debt

While living debt free is ideal, most people carry some debt in the form of credit cards, mortgages, and other loans. It is important that you take the time to analyze your debt situation and determine whether it is under control. You should also pull a copy of your credit report and see where you stand.

There are many strategies for managing debt. They range from systematically paying down credit card balances and substituting expensive, high-interest debt with lower cost options, to negotiating directly with your creditors to reduce or eliminate balances. A debt financial advisor can help you devise a plan appropriate for your situation.

Updating Your Estate Plan

I should title this section "What You Want to Have Happen to Your Stuff Once You Are Gone" because that's what estate planning is all about. Of course there are tax strategies and a whole bunch of other things like trusts that are part of it but, at its most basic level, it is what happens to your assets after you are no longer with the living.

Estate planning is often ignored, sometimes for years, following a divorce. Yet, failing to address it right away can have disastrous consequences. Yes, it usually requires a lawyer, and you are probably tired of them; it can be dry and boring…but it is oh so important to deal with.

Your post-divorce estate plan breaks down into three main areas:

- Updating beneficiaries and account ownership
- Creating wills and trusts
- Creating living wills and other end-of-life directives

Update Beneficiaries and Account Ownership

Most people think of wills and trusts as the documents that direct where their assets go after they die. For many people this is not true! That is because many accounts and assets already have beneficiaries designated. These include:

- 💰 IRAs

- 💰 401(k) and other retirement plans

- 💰 Jointly owned property

- 💰 Transfer-on-death accounts

- 💰 Annuities

- 💰 Assets held in a trust.

Each one of these accounts will bypass your will if there is a named person as beneficiary. The account owners need to update them if they want a different beneficiary.

Update Wills and Trusts

Wills and trusts are the core documents you need in order to distribute the assets without designated beneficiaries as noted above.

A *will* is also the document where you can designate your children's guardian in case your ex-spouse is not available and specify the executor of your estate.

A *revocable living trust* is another way to direct who receives the assets in your estate. Its main benefit is that the settlement of your estate will be a private matter not subject to the public probate process. Assets held in the name of the trust (like your home and taxable investment accounts) are subject to the terms of the trust. All other assets flow through your will, which you will have in addition to your trust.

A revocable living trust is not to be confused with other types of trusts that are used to reduce estate and income taxes, give away assets while you are alive in a tax advantaged way, or for any number of other purposes.

You should meet with a lawyer to review your unique circumstances and see if a will or revocable living trust is best suited for your unique circumstances and desires. Not everyone needs a revocable living trust.

Create Living Wills and Health Care Proxies

As you create your will or trust you will want to create documents that specify what happens should you become incapacitated and can't make decisions for yourself. These documents fall into two basic categories: living wills and health care proxies.

A *living will* expresses how you want to be treated in certain medical circumstances. Depending on your state's laws, it may permit you to convey whether you wish to be given life-sustaining treatment if you are terminally ill or injured.

A *health care proxy*, also known as a durable medical power of attorney, is a document that specifically grants someone the authority to make medical decisions for you in the event you can't speak for yourself.

Taxes

What follows is not to be construed as tax advice since I'm not an accountant. But what I can say emphatically is that you will want to consult one!

It is important to know that your tax situation will change now that you are divorced. You will need to address:

- 💰 Changing your filing status from "married" to either "single" or "head of household." In general the determining factor is whether you were married or single as of December 31.

- 💰 Working with your ex-spouse and accountant to decide who will take various child deductions and exemptions. This may already have been agreed upon as part of your settlement.

- 💰 Accounting for asset sales. You might have to pay taxes on the proceeds of home sales and sales of investments that occurred in the process of implementing your property settlement.

On your personal recovery action sheet you should make a note to *schedule an appointment with an accountant at your first opportunity.* Do not wait for next year's tax filing season, since you will want to fully understand your unique tax situation and develop strategies for minimizing your tax bill.

Actions to Take Now

- 💰 Gather your data and create your spending plan.

- Meet with an attorney and update your estate plan. Make decisions on whether any kind of trusts are required or whether a simple will is adequate.

- Review all beneficiary data and update

- Meet with an accountant and discuss your tax strategy as a single person.

CHAPTER 25

Creating Your Personal Investment And Insurance Program

"If you don't know where you are going,
you'll end up someplace else."
—*Yogi Berra*

O nce the dust has settled and you are on your own, you will want to get down to the business of building an investment and insurance strategy that supports your goals as an independent person.

This chapter describes the steps to take to assess your portfolio and make adjustments that are right for you and also how to approach the task of acquiring the proper amount and type of insurance coverage.

Your Life Has Changed—So Should Your Investment Strategy

The assets you received as part of your divorce settlement may be a hodgepodge of retirement accounts, cash, and other investments that are inappropriate for your new life. You have a unique set of financial needs for supporting your lifestyle, saving for retirement, buying your own home, educating kids and many others. They are your goals, so you need to have a portfolio that is *yours*.

Find a Qualified Advisor

Divorce is a life event where most people can benefit from the expertise of a qualified financial advisor.

There are many people in the "wealth management" business, and like any other profession there are some who are more qualified than others. Ideally, the person you choose will be a fee-based specialist in divorce financial planning and not just a product salesperson.

Speak with people you trust and interview at least two recommended advisors. Choose the one with the credentials, experience, and demeanor that resonate with you. It is essential they have an ability to listen and communicate, and they must be able to clearly explain their fees and their approach to managing your investments.

You should expect a comprehensive analysis of your investments and a written plan that documents your goals, defines your investment strategy, and gives you specific recommendations and action steps.

Start at the Beginning

As Glinda the Good Witch said, "It is always best to start at the beginning," and in personal finance that means understanding the portfolio you own today. Ask your advisor to prepare a formal portfolio analysis and start down your own yellow brick road. You should learn about your portfolio's composition, performance, risk, and cost.

Your Portfolio Composition or 'Asset Allocation'

Understanding your portfolio begins with your asset allocation—that is, the ratio of stocks, bonds, and cash. Studies show that your return and risk over time is largely dependent on the percentages you have in each of these categories. It is the first conversation you need to have with your advisor about your portfolio's design.

Performance History

It is a truism that past performance is not an indicator of future results, but you should still know whether your portfolio has generated positive returns for you.

Performance should be evaluated not just in absolute terms (what your portfolio gained or lost), but also how it performed relative to the markets as a whole and how specific investments you own, like mutual funds, performed relative to others in their category.

Risk

You will want to know how "risky" your portfolio is. There are many risks to consider, but what most people care about is how susceptible the portfolio is to the ups and downs of the stock and bond markets. Your advisor should be able to show you how the portfolio as a whole fared when the markets suffered a pullback and the risk profile of each investment.

Common Portfolio Mistakes

Investing Cash You May Need to Spend Soon

We are discussing in this chapter your long-term investments, i.e., money that you are not going to touch for at least five years. Ideally, you should have six months' worth of expenses in cash set aside for daily living.

Your Portfolio Isn't Part of an Overall Wealth Plan

Portfolios need to be built around your life. Your needs for growth, safety, and income all should be considered along with your "time horizon," meaning how long the money can stay in place before being spent. Jimmy's college fund that will be needed in three years should be invested differently than a retirement account that won't be tapped for fifteen years.

Your Portfolio Is Not Diversified

It is generally a bad idea, a very bad idea, to have your portfolio dominated by one stock, or even one industry. Whether it is your employer's stock in your 401(k), a stock purchase plan, or the GE stock Aunt Tootie left you, if you have too much of your nest egg in one firm you will suffer should things should go wrong. And if it is also your employer, you could risk losing your job *and* your savings should the company go through a tough time.

Your portfolio needs to be diversified across different types of securities, not just stock investments. A properly risk-managed portfolio will contain bonds, cash, and other assets not subject to the whims of the stock market.

Paying Too Much in Fees

Fees are *everywhere* in portfolios. While most people focus on the advisory fee charged by the investment professional, they routinely ignore the costs of the investments themselves. As an example, the average mutual fund expense is 1.2 percent. You pay that each year regardless of how it performs or whether you use an advisor.

Some actively managed mutual funds (where someone is being paid to buy and sell securities for the fund) are worth their fee. As a group, however, most mutual funds do not do better than low-cost "index" portfolios that simply track the overall market and whose costs are as low as 0.2 percent.

Buying Expensive Insurance Products You May Not Need

In recent years there has been an explosion of insurance-based investment products designed to give you various income or growth "guarantees" for an additional fee. They may have a role in your retirement planning but should not be used as the foundation for your core portfolio. They are also the most expensive products to own because you are paying an additional 1.5 to 3 percent per year for the insurance features of these contracts and often have penalties for removing funds within the first few years.

Setting It and Forgetting It

A portfolio that is ignored and never adjusted can be dangerous to your financial health. At least once a year it needs to be reviewed and "rebalanced" so that it stays true to the original portfolio design. And if market conditions change significantly, or if your financial circumstances change, it should be modified in a prudent fashion.

Creating an Insurance Program Right for You

Just the word "insurance" is enough to make some people want to run in the other direction. The fact is that insurance is something most people need in one form or another. It is a unique product that has the ability to give you and your family protection from death, major illness, and a host of other life events that could otherwise threaten your financial health.

Chances are you will need to do *something* with the policies that were in place during your marriage. You may need to simply modify an existing policy so that it gives the proper amount of coverage to the proper beneficiary, or you may need to start from scratch.

Insurance salespeople do not have a reputation for excitement (recall Woody Allen from chapter 19), but they are true professionals who can help you evaluate your requirements and recommend the best mix of policies for you. If you are working with a financial coach, he or she can refer you to people who understand divorce financial recovery and will put your interests first.

There are several kinds of insurance to consider. You may need all or some depending on your circumstances.

Life Insurance

A better name for this is "death insurance." It is used to protect you and your family should an income provider die.

Ask yourself the following question: "What will happen to my financial life and my family's security if I die?" (Or, if someone you rely on for income or future financial support dies.)

- 💰 Will I be able to retire when I want to?

- 💰 Will my children be able to go to college?

- 💰 Will I be able to support myself and maintain my standard of living?

If the answer is "no" to any of these questions, then it is likely you will want life insurance.

As Part of Your Marital Settlement

If you are counting on child support or alimony for a substantial part of your income, you may have made arrangements for your spouse to carry life insurance so that those payments will continue on should he or she die. Or you may have negotiated that they carry a policy to cover education commitments or let you pay off the mortgage so your children can stay in the family home.

As mentioned in chapter 23 in the section "Dissecting and Monitoring Your Agreement," you need to monitor those commitments to make sure they are carried out and stay in place over time as part of your recovery action plan.

As New Coverage

A proper risk analysis by a qualified insurance professional will tell you whether you need life insurance to create new or supplemental income should you die.

There are many types of insurance—too many to go into in detail here...but they break down into two basic categories:

- 💰 insurance which simply pays you an amount at death (term insurance)

- 💰 insurance with a savings (cash value) component in addition to the death payment (whole and universal life insurance)

Most people choose term insurance when there is a need for insurance for a limited period of time and when they don't desire any kind of investment or savings vehicle. Term insurance is the lowest cost way to gain coverage, although it costs more as you get older.

Whole life and universal life insurance pay out a death benefit but extra money is paid into the policy each year to be credited to an account that potentially grows in value each year. These are complicated policies that you need to evaluate carefully. Take your time to make sure you understand the details.

Health Insurance

If your ex-spouse provided health care coverage for the family through his or her employer, you may or may not have negotiated to maintain that coverage in the future. Or you may have had them agree to pay for your own policy as part of your settlement.

Regardless, it is critical that you *not have a lapse in coverage*. There are three ways to acquire health insurance.

Continuing Coverage Under Your Ex-Spouse's Employer Plan

Many states, like Massachusetts, have laws that allow divorced spouses to stay on their ex-husband or wife's policy provided by their employer.

It is important to understand your state's laws regarding whether your spouse's employer is obligated to cover you once your divorce is finalized. If the law allows, you may find your lowest cost and simplest option is to stay on your ex's health plan.

COBRA

No, it's not a snake. It is shorthand for the federal act that allows you to pick up coverage provided by an employer plan at group rates for a limited period of time. If you cannot be covered under an employer plan as a result of your divorce, then you have the opportunity to buy into the group plan, although the employer will not subsidize your payment.

Look into your state's laws as noted above, and refer to the US Department of Labor website to learn more about COBRA.

Affordable Care Act (Obamacare) Insurance Marketplace

With the passage of the Affordable Care Act, also known as Obamacare, many people who in the past would have been shut out of the marketplace can now acquire health insurance. You may be able to get reduced health care premiums for you and your family depending on your income. Divorce is one of the events that make you eligible to sign up for insurance after the annual deadline.

More information can be found at healthcare.gov.

Actions to Take Now

- Gather your investment and insurance statements. For insurance also get a copy of the contract, which will give you details about each policy. You may need to go to your or your spouse's employer or to the insurance company directly to get what you need.

- Interview at least two insurance and investment professionals and select one with the qualifications and demeanor that matches your needs and personality. A financial coach can help you locate qualified candidates.

- Have your chosen advisor(s) analyze your requirements and your current investments and insurance, and prepare recommendations for your approval.

- If you are working with a financial coach they will be meeting with you regularly to help you track all of the activities documented on the personal financial action plan you built together. His or her job is to help you stay on track and move you down the path to financial recovery.

CHAPTER 26

Achieving the Fresh Start You Deserve

*"Sometimes good things fall apart
so that better things can fall together."*
—Marilyn Monroe

You have created your vision, negotiated your settlement, and developed your recovery action plan. Now it is time to put the plan in place and get on with your new life.

Following Through on Your Plan Is Like Eating an Elephant

If you follow my guidance on developing a personal financial action plan, you have a lot words on paper and intentions at this point. Now it is just a "small" matter of acting on them. Like eating the proverbial elephant one bite at a time, you need to take it in small pieces.

That is why we have created a calendar of tasks; the most urgent get dealt with first and those less important are deferred for a while. You will have a flurry of activity as you deal with the urgent administrative tasks we have outlined, but that will subside as you systematically begin checking those tasks off your list. It is a wonderful feeling to see the list of to-do's get smaller and smaller, and it will help you get a feeling of progress and renew your energy.

Your Advisor as Sherpa

Way back in the beginning of this book I described the need for a divorce Sherpa, someone to guide you up the divorce mountain. It is an apt metaphor for the role of your financial coach as you implement your plan. It is your plan, your mountain, but your advisor is there to create a path for you to follow, helping you link up with the right professionals, think through important decisions, and stay on course.

Check-in Meetings

Once your plan is established there will not be a need for frequent conversations. But you will still want to have formal check-in meetings, either in person or on the phone, to discuss progress on your plan. I recommend at least monthly discussions, but these can be more or less frequent depending on the complexity of your plan.

Your CDFA™ will help you stay focused, ferret out the answers to issues that arise, and act as a sounding board about your concerns.

Ongoing Support

Once you have completed your personal financial action plan there will be less need to talk with your CDFA™. But he or she remains available for you as one of your trusted advisors should the need arise. Depending on the nature of the practice, he or she may have other services you can take advantage of.

Take Time for Recovery

It is easy to get overwhelmed with the many choices you have, and a financial coach can help simplify your decision-making, saving you time and making sure your plan comes together properly. It is the reason they are called a "financial ally."

But I think it is important to note that an emotional life coach may also be helpful. I am not a therapist, but the research is clear that losing a marriage, regardless of the circumstances, is like having a death in the family. It takes time to process it all, even if you are relieved to be single again.

So, as you go through this new stage of life, I leave you with some of the things I learned going through my own divorce, and from observing the divorces of my friends and clients.

I present to you "Licciardello's Personal Rules of Divorce Recovery":

- Do things that give you joy, every day...don't defer them
- Surround yourself with uplifting people

- 💰 Seek out a counselor to help you get through the rough spots

- 💰 Nurture your spiritual side

- 💰 Focus on yourself and your family first

- 💰 Don't be in a rush to find a serious relationship

- 💰 Be kind to your body and give it the respect it deserves

- 💰 Give yourself time to let change happen at its own pace

- 💰 Take comfort in knowing that you will experience love and feel normal again.

Divorce is difficult, but it passes. It takes time to feel like your old self again, but you will get there.

I hope you have taken something of value from this little book. It is my first one and I am sure it can be improved. Please send me your comments at wentworthplanning@gmail.com, and feel free to ask me questions.

Oh, by the way, my friend Sheila—whom I described in the beginning of this book—is doing fine. She is resettled in a home of her own, found work she really loves, and met a good man who also went through a nasty divorce experience. She is taking it slow but feels they might have a future together. And she is still a friend of mine.

Helpful Tools

Preparation

Comparison of Mediation, Collaboration and Litigation

Financial Readiness Scorecard

Scorecard Assessment Questions

Vision

Lifestyle and Vision Questions

Developing Your Vision

Your Personal Action Plan

Getting organized

Documents and Data Gathering Checklist

Creating Your Game Plan

Must-Haves and Like-to-Haves

Financial Strengths and Weaknesses

Negotiation Stage

Five-Year Net Worth and Income Projection

Before and After Income Summary

Recovery

Personal Recovery Action Plan

Divorce: Mediation vs. Collaborative vs. Litigation

	Mediation	Collaborative	Litigation
Who Controls the Process	You and your spouse control the process and make final decisions	You and your spouse control the process and make final decisions	Judge controls the process and makes final decisions
Degree of Adversity	You and your spouse pledge openness	You and your spouse pledge mutual respect and openness	Court process is based on an adversarial system
Cost	Costs are manageable, usually less expensive than litigation	Costs are manageable, usually less expensive than litigation; team model is financially efficient in use of professionals	Costs are unpredictable and can escalate rapidly including frequency of post-judgment litigation
Timetable	You and your spouse create the timetable	You and your spouse create the timetable	Judge sets the timetable; often delays given crowded court
Use of Outside Experts	Use of outside experts is limited but they can be involved as needed	Jointly retained specialists provide information and guidance helping you and your spouse develop informed, mutually beneficial solutions	Separate experts are hired to support the litigants' positions, often at great expense to each
Involvement of Lawyers	Lawyers typically do not participate directly in mediation sessions, but are consulted between sessions	Lawyers work toward a mutually created settlement	Lawyers fight to win, but someone loses
Privacy	The process, discussion and negotiation details are kept private	The process, discussion and negotiation details are kept private	Dispute becomes a matter of public record and, sometimes, media attention
Facilitation of Communication	Mediator facilitates communication during sessions	Team of Collaborative Practice specialists educate and assist you and your spouse on how to effectively communicate with each other	No process designed to facilitate communication
Voluntary vs. Mandatory	Voluntary	Voluntary	Mandatory if no agreement
Lines of Communication	You and your spouse communicate directly with the assistance of mediator	You and your spouse communicate directly with the assistance of members of your team	You and your spouse negotiate through lawyers
Children's Participation	Children are not directly involved	Children are interviewed by the Child Specialist professional who helps the parents discuss the children's needs	A lawyer appointed as guardian *ad litem* interviews children and makes a recommendation to the Judge
Court Involvement	Outside court	Outside court	Court-based

This comparison table has been adapted from materials in the Collaborative Divorce Knowledge Kit provided by the International Academy of Collaborative Professionals and available at www.collaborativepractice.com

The Fresh
Start Program™

The Divorce Financial
Readiness Scorecard

I do not have a clear vision of my post-divorce life.	1	2	3	4	5	6	7	8	9	10	I have a clear, well-defined vision of my post-divorce life.
I do not fully understand all aspects of my family's personal finances.	1	2	3	4	5	6	7	8	9	10	I fully understand all aspects of my family's personal finances.
I do not know how much money I will need to live on after my divorce.	1	2	3	4	5	6	7	8	9	10	I know exactly how much money I will need to live on after my divorce.
I do not understand how my divorce may affect my retirement, estate and investment strategy.	1	2	3	4	5	6	7	8	9	10	I understand exactly how my divorce may affect my retirement, estate and investment strategy.
I have no idea what I should want most in my divorce financial settlement.	1	2	3	4	5	6	7	8	9	10	I know exactly what I should want most in my divorce financial settlement.
I don't feel confident I can properly evaluate proposals offered during negotiations.	1	2	3	4	5	6	7	8	9	10	I feel very confident I can properly evaluate proposals offered during negotiations.
I do not know what to do to get my finances in complete order after my divorce.	1	2	3	4	5	6	7	8	9	10	I know exactly what to do to get my finances in complete order after my divorce.
I feel stressed and worried about my situation.	1	2	3	4	5	6	7	8	9	10	I feel very confident and relaxed about my situation.
I am worried about how my divorce will affect the relationships important to me, especially my children.	1	2	3	4	5	6	7	8	9	10	I am confident that I will be able to take care all of the relationships important to me, especially my children.
I do not feel excited and confident that I will enjoy my life fully after my divorce.	1	2	3	4	5	6	7	8	9	10	I feel excited and confident that I will enjoy my life fully after my divorce.

Your Scorecard Total: _____

1. Why did you give yourself that score? 2. What do you need to do to improve your score?

What is Your Financial Readiness?

What were your three lowest scoring areas?

1. _____
2. _____
3. _____

What is needed to score higher in each?

1. _____
2. _____
3. _____

How would the FreshStart Program benefit you most?

1. _____
2. _____
3. _____

Lifestyle and Vision Questions

IDENTIFYING WHAT IS MOST IMPORTANT TO YOU

Your living situation
- Where do you anticipate living after your divorce?
- What is most important to you in your future living situation?
- Do you desire to stay in the marital residence?
- Do you anticipate keeping the family home?
- Where do you see your children living? With you only? Shared?
- Do you anticipate staying in the local area after your children are no longer minors?

Your work
- What would you do for work if you could have your ideal job?
- What are your career plans after your divorce?
- Are you planning on getting new training or education? If so, for how long?
- Do you anticipate receiving or providing spousal income support (i.e., alimony)

Your children
- What is your ideal vision of how your children will live and feel after your divorce?
- What concerns do you have for your children's well being?

Your spouse
- What kind of relationship do you want with your ex-spouse?
- What is your vision of how you would co-parent with your spouse?

Relationships
- How do you see your divorce affecting your relationship with family, friends, children?
- How important is it to you to protect and preserve relationships?
- What do you see as necessary to maintain those relationships during and after your divorce?

Retirement vision
- What does retirement look like to you?
- What is your anticipated retirement date? Will you retire completely or simply work less?
- What hobbies would you like to pursue if you had more time and no money worries?

Other goals
- What other long term goals do you have?
    - Personal, career, and other...
    - For your children

Developing Your Vision

The Vision Questions

Write down in detail exactly what you would be doing, and how you would be feeling, if you were fully enjoying all aspects of your life following your divorce

Lifestyle

_____
_____
_____
_____

Relationships

_____
_____
_____
_____

Long Term Goals/Other

_____
_____
_____
_____
_____

Your Personal Action Plan

Name of Vision_____

The Three Projects

To achieve my Vision, I need to work on these three projects:

1.

2.

3.

My Three Actions

To get started, I must immediately take these three actions:

1.

2.

3.

Getting Organized

DOCUMENTS AND DATA GATHERING CHECKLIST

Cash Assets
Checking and savings accounts ⎯⎯⎯⎯
Brokerage based money market accounts ⎯⎯⎯⎯

Income and Deductions
Recent paystubs with deduction data ⎯⎯⎯⎯

Investment and Retirement Accounts
Brokerage accounts ⎯⎯⎯⎯
IRAs and variable annuities ⎯⎯⎯⎯
College 529 plans ⎯⎯⎯⎯
Custodial accounts for children ⎯⎯⎯⎯

Corporate Based Assets and Benefits
401(k) and profit sharing plans ⎯⎯⎯⎯
Stock option and stock purchase plans ⎯⎯⎯⎯
Deferred compensation ⎯⎯⎯⎯
Pension plans ⎯⎯⎯⎯
Corporate life and disability insurance ⎯⎯⎯⎯
Health care plan information ⎯⎯⎯⎯

Debt
Personal loans ⎯⎯⎯⎯
Credit cards ⎯⎯⎯⎯
Mortgage and home equity loans ⎯⎯⎯⎯

Insurance
Term insurance contracts ⎯⎯⎯⎯
Whole life and universal life insurance contracts ⎯⎯⎯⎯

Estate Planning Documents
Wills and trust documents ⎯⎯⎯⎯
Guardianship papers ⎯⎯⎯⎯
Health care proxies ⎯⎯⎯⎯

Personal Property
Real estate and rental property ⎯⎯⎯⎯
Vehicles ⎯⎯⎯⎯
Other personal property ⎯⎯⎯⎯

Assessing Your Financial Strengths and Weaknesses

Using the guidelines and questions found in chapter 9 to make a note below of the major strengths and weaknesses of your personal finances.

My top 5 personal financial *strengths* are

1. _____
2. _____
3. _____
4. _____
5. _____

My top 5 personal financial *weaknesses* are

1. _____
2. _____
3. _____
4. _____
5. _____

Other Issues

1. _____
2. _____

Your "Must Haves" and "Like To Haves"

Write below what you feel you must absolutely have in your post-divorce lifestyle and settlement agreement to be minimally acceptable, and what you would like to have but feel is negotiable.

"Must haves"

1. _____
2. _____
3. _____
4. _____
5. _____
6. _____
7. _____
8. _____

"Like to Haves"

1. _____
2. _____
3. _____
4. _____
5. _____
6. _____
7. _____
8. _____

The FreshStart Recovery
Personal Financial Action Plan

The Fresh
Start Program™

Action item	When	Status	Complete ✓
Putting Your Agreement in Place			
Review agreement			
Create master action item			
Receiving Assets			
Open accounts in your name			
Assets received			
Checking Savings			
Investment Account			
IRA Accounts			
Ex-Spouse Employer Retirement Plans			
QDRO's Created			
QDRO's Sent to employer			
QDRO's acted on by employer			
Accounts opened to receive assets			
Assets received			
Other Employer Plans			
Pension information			
Stock option vesting schedule			
Stock purchase plan documentation			
Budgeting			
Create a budget			
Develop savings plan			
Your Investments			
Gather account statements			
Review employer retirement plans			
Conduct portfolio analysis			
Create written strategy			
Retirement			
Education Funding			
Open Accounts			
Transfer Assets			

The FreshStart Recovery
Personal Financial Action Plan

 The **Fresh**
Start Program™

Action item	When	Status	Complete ✓
Your Estate Plan			
Gather copies of wills, trusts etc...			
Document review and assessment			
Select attorney			
Select an executor			
Select guardian			
Prepare Documents			
Will/Trust			
Guardianship			
Living will			
Health Care Proxy			
Authorize Documents			
Update beneficiary designations			
Insurance			
IRA/401(k)			
Retitle Assets			

Action item	When	Status	Complete ✓
Insurance and Risk Management			
Gather existing insurance contracts			
Review Contracts			
Conduct Needs Analysis			
Develop recommendations			
Solicit new quotes			
Life			
Health			
Property			
Other			

Action item	When	Status	Complete ✓
Credit			
Close joint credit card accounts			
Open new credit card accounts			
Get Credit Score Report			
Review mortgage for refinancing			
Taxes			
Consult with CPA regarding filing status			
Update withholding if needed			

Five Year Projection

Projections for George J Jones and Marianne P Jones.

This table shows key income, expense and tax results projected for years, 1, 2, 3, 4, and 5.
The graph below shows net worth projected for 10 years.

# Years	1	2	3	4	5
Year	2016	2017	2018	2019	2020
Total Income					
George	$184,900	$188,397	$192,110	$195,939	$200,313
Marianne	$103,896	$105,295	$105,969	$88,663	$86,642
Total Expenses					
George	$126,244	$127,565	$128,984	$112,402	$110,862
Marianne	$81,821	$108,632	$110,596	$112,638	$116,894
Total Taxes					
George	$58,476	$53,148	$54,251	$59,271	$60,541
Marianne	$10,604	$11,333	$12,027	$11,199	$11,423
Net Income After Expenses and Taxes					
George	$180	$7,684	$8,875	$24,266	$28,910
Marianne	$11,471	($14,670)	($16,654)	($35,174)	($41,675)
Year-End Net Worth					
George	$243,862	$270,991	$300,800	$347,633	$401,388
Marianne	$285,348	$307,048	$326,943	$331,031	$331,123

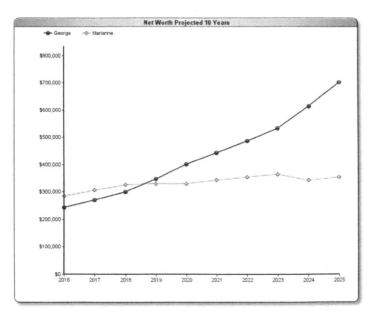

Illustration courtesy of Family Law Software

Income Summary Report - Annual - 2016 Actual

		George	Marianne
1.	Income..................	184,900	51,900
2.	Child Support..............	(39,996)	39,996
3.	Alimony...................	(12,000)	12,000
4.	Inc aft suppt (lns 1 to 3).......	132,904	103,896
5.	Total taxes & mand exp.......	58,476	10,604
6.	Inc After Taxes (4-5).........	74,428	93,292
7.	% of Combined..............	44	56
8.	Living Expenses.............	74,248	81,821
9.	Net Aft Tax & Exp............	180	11,471

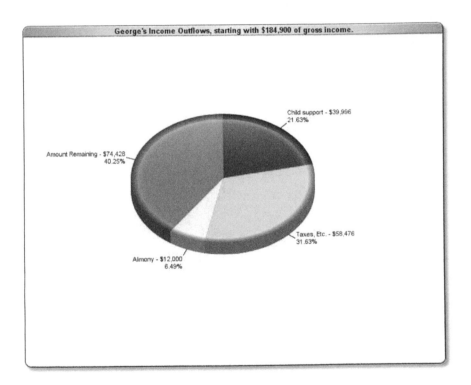

George's Income Outflows, starting with $184,900 of gross income.

Child support - $39,996
21.63%

Amount Remaining - $74,428
40.25%

Taxes, Etc. - $58,476
31.63%

Alimony - $12,000
6.49%

Illustration courtesy of Family Law Software

Index

About the Author

J. A. Licciardello is the founder of Wentworth Divorce Consultants and creator of the FreshStart Program™. Along with other affiliated financial specialists he helps couples navigate the financial maze of divorce so they can live the life they want.

Mr. Licciardello has been practicing financial planning and helping solve financial issues for over twenty years. He has had extensive training as a financial planner and additional credentials as a *Certified Divorce Financial Analyst* (CDFA™), which gives him specialized knowledge in the field of divorce financial planning. He also has extensive training in mediation and collaborative divorce and has written numerous articles in the field of divorce finance.

J. A. Licciardello holds a bachelor's degree from the University of Maryland, and a master's in business administration from the University of Connecticut. Prior to his financial services career he was a manager at IBM and former President of the Financial Planning Association of Rhode Island.

He lives in New England with his three children, and when he isn't sailing enjoys writing music, cooking, and gardening.

Contacting J. A. Licciardello

The author works with couples and individuals going through divorce as a Certified Divorce Financial Analyst and mediator. His private practice, located in southern New England, consults with divorcing clients and attorneys across the United States helping them create ideal settlements and avoid financial mistakes.

He can be reached at 401-533-4142, or via email at wentworth planning@gmail.com.

Made in the USA
Middletown, DE
10 December 2019